Mastering Tai Chi Form 24 and Applications

with Double-Clubbell, Cane, and Long Staff

簡化太極拳24式與衍生的雙棒-拐杖-長棍

A Note to the Reader

This book includes four complete and practical routines:

Simplified Tai Chi Form 24
Tai Chi Double-Clubbell/Bang in Form 24
Tai Chi Cane in Form 24
Tai Chi Long Staff in Form 24

To assist your learning, the author has created companion instructional DVDs/videos demonstrating each of these routines. Please note: these videos are not included with the book purchase but are available separately at:

https://taichihealthways.com/all-dvds

You can also preview selected video content on the author's YouTube channel:

https://www.youtube.com/@taichitsao

Jesse Tsao 曹鳳山博士, PhD

Tai Chi Healthways
Summer, 2025

© Copyright 2025 Jesse Tsao, PhD; Published by Tai Chi Healthways

www.taichihealthways.com

All rights reserved. Intended for personal use only. No part of this publication may be reproduced, stored in a retrieval system, or transmitted, in any form or by any means. Electronic, mechanical, photocopied, recorded or otherwise, without prior permission in writing from the publisher.

ISBN: 978-1-7361961-8-2 (Paperback)

ALL RIGHTS RESERVED

Printed in the U.S.A

Chief Editor: Valneva Puiger

Book Designer: Heidi Sutherlin

Interior Photographs: Jennifer Tsao

Cover photo: Penglai Temple in Dr. Jesse Tsao's hometown, Penglai, China
中國蓬萊閣 courtesy of Dr. Xu Tai-yong 攝影家徐太勇

Disclaimer: The author recommends that you consult your physician regarding the applicability of any recommendations and follow all safety instructions before beginning any exercise program. When participating in any exercise or exercise program, there is the possibility of physical injury. You agree that you do so at your own risk, and are voluntarily participating in these activities.

For Professor Li Deyin 李德印教授, *with respect and admiration*

The Wushu Team of Beijing Renmin University of China

1980, Beijing

Professor Li Deyin – Coach 李德印教練, 4th from the left (back row)

Dr. Jesse Tsao – Author of this book 著者曹鳳山博士,
5th from the left (front row)

風華正茂
武術同門四十五年前

In our youthful prime -
Wushu family forty-five years ago

"Your concept and creation effectively balance tradition, innovation, safety, and convenience, reflecting the spirit of maintaining authenticity while embracing creativity."

你的構思和創編很好解決了傳統，新穎，安全，方便的矛盾，體現了守正創新的精神.

– Professor Li Deyin

Contents

Acknowledgements 1

Introduction 7

Part I: Illustrated Simplified Tai Chi Form 24 — 15

Posture 1: Opening Form 16
Posture 2: Part Wild Horse's Mane 18
Posture 3: White Crane Spreading Its Wings 23
Posture 4: Brush Knee on Both Sides 25
Posture 5: Playing a Guitar 28
Posture 6: Repulse Monkey 29
Posture 7: Grasp the Bird's Tail - Left 33
Posture 8: Grasp the Bird's Tail - Right 36
Posture 9: Single Whip 38
Posture 10: Wave Hands Like Clouds 40
Posture 11: Single Whip 43
Posture 12: High Pat on Horse 44
Posture 13: Kick with Right Heel 46
Posture 14: Strike Opponent's Ears with Both Fists 49
Posture 15: Kick with Left Heel 51
Posture 16: Golden Rooster Stands on One Leg - Left 52
Posture 17: Golden Rooster Stands on One Leg - Right 54
Posture 18: Fair Lady Works with Shuttles on Both Sides 55
Posture 19: Needle at Sea Bottom 57
Posture 20: Fan Through the Back 59
Posture 21: Turn to Deflect, Parry and Punch 61
Posture 22: Apparent Closure 64
Posture 23: Cross Hands 65
Posture 24: Closing Form 67

Part II: Tai Chi Double-Clubbell in Form 24 — 71

- Posture 1: Opening Form 71
- Posture 2: Part Wild Horse's Mane 73
- Posture 3: White Crane Spreading Its Wings.....................................75
- Posture 4: Brush Knee on Both Sides 76
- Posture 5: Playing a Guitar 78
- Posture 6: Repulse Monkey 79
- Posture 7: Grasp the Bird's Tail - Left 82
- Posture 8: Grasp the Bird's Tail - Right 84
- Posture 9: Single Whip...86
- Posture 10: Wave Hands Like Clouds 88
- Posture 11: Single Whip...90
- Posture 12: High Pat on Horse 91
- Posture 13: Kick with Right Heel..92
- Posture 14: Strike Opponent's Ears with Both Fists 94
- Posture 15: Kick with Left Heel..95
- Posture 16: Golden Rooster Stands on One Leg - Left 96
- Posture 17: Golden Rooster Stands on One Leg - Right 98
- Posture 18: Fair Lady Works with Shuttles on Both Sides 99
- Posture 19: Needle at Sea Bottom 101
- Posture 20: Fan Through the Back 102
- Posture 21: Turn to Deflect, Parry and Punch.................................103
- Posture 22: Apparent Closure 105
- Posture 23: Cross Hands 106
- Posture 24: Closing Form 107

Part III: Tai Chi Cane in Simplified Form 24 — 111

- Posture 1: Opening Form 111
- Posture 2: Part Wild Horse's Mane 113
- Posture 3: White Crane Spreading Its Wings...................................116
- Posture 4: Brush Knee on Both Sides 118
- Posture 5: Playing a Guitar..121
- Posture 6: Repulse Monkey 122
- Posture 7: Grasp the Bird's Tail - Left 125
- Posture 8: Grasp the Bird's Tail - Right 128
- Posture 9: Single Whip...131
- Posture 10: Wave Hands Like Clouds 133

Posture 11: Single Whip 140
Posture 12: High Pat on Horse 142
Posture 13: Kick with Right Heel..143
Posture 14: Strike Opponent's Ears with Both Fists 145
Posture 15: Kick with Left Heel..146
Posture 16: Golden Rooster Stands on One Leg -Left 148
Posture 17: Golden Rooster Stands on One Leg - Right 151
Posture 18: Fair Lady Works with Shuttles on Both Sides 153
Posture 19: Needle at Sea Bottom 156
Posture 20: Fan Through the Back 158
Posture 21: Turn to Deflect, Parry and Punch............................159
Posture 22: Apparent Closure 161
Posture 23: Cross Hands 162
Posture 24: Closing Form 163

Part IV: Tai Chi Long Staff in Simplified Form 24   167

Posture 1: Opening Form 167
Posture 2: Part Wild Horse's Mane..168
Posture 3: White Crane Spreading Its Wings.............................172
Posture 4: Brush Knee on Both Sides...174
Posture 5: Playing a Guitar..178
Posture 6: Repulse Monkey...180
Posture 7: Grasp the Bird's Tail - Left...184
Posture 8: Grasp the Bird's Tail - Right 187
Posture 9: Single Whip..190
Posture 10: Wave Hands Like Clouds 193
Posture 11: Single Whip 200
Posture 12: High Pat on Horse 201
Posture 13: Kick with Right Heel..202
Posture 14: Strike Opponent's Ears with Both Fists 204
Posture 15: Kick with Left Heel..206
Posture 16: Golden Rooster Stands on One Leg - Left 208
Posture 17: Golden Rooster Stands on One Leg - Right.........212
Posture 18: Fair Lady Works with Shuttles on Both Sides 214
Posture 19: Needle at Sea Bottom 217
Posture 20: Fan Through the Back 218
Posture 21: Turn to Deflect, Parry and Punch............................219

Posture 22: Apparent Closure 221
Posture 23: Cross Hands 223
Posture 24: Closing Form 225

Supplement 229
Simplified Tai Chi Form 24 Wall Chart 簡化太極拳掛圖 1956 229

About the Author 233

Acknowledgements

I would like to begin by dedicating this book to Professor Li Deyin (李德印) of Renmin University of China in Beijing — a legendary figure and global pioneer in the instruction and promotion of the Simplified Tai Chi Form 24.

From 1978 to 1987, I had the great privilege of studying under his guidance. Those formative years laid the foundation for my lifelong journey in Tai Chi, shaping not only my technical understanding but also my appreciation for the art's rich cultural and philosophical dimensions.

Professor Li is more than a coach — he is a guiding light. As the third generation in his family to teach Tai Chi professionally, he carries a remarkable legacy. His uncle, Li Tianji (李天驥), was the head coach of the martial arts program at the Chinese Central Sports Institute and the primary author and demonstrator of the Simplified Tai Chi Form 24. Building on this lineage, Professor Li has continued to expand and share Tai Chi with unrelenting dedication. His commitment is matched by a profound passion for education. He has always inspired his students not only to master the form but to become stewards of the tradition — to teach, to innovate, and to serve the greater good through Tai Chi.

I still vividly remember the words he once shared with me:

"繼承發揚太極拳，造福人民大眾。"

"Inherit and carry forward Tai Chi, and bring its benefits to the people."

This simple yet profound message has stayed with me throughout my life and served as a guiding principle during the writing of this book. His influence runs through every chapter, and I remain deeply grateful for his teachings, encouragement, and enduring vision.

I have also been privileged to study with many extraordinary masters throughout my Tai Chi journey. Their profound knowledge and personal guidance have left a lasting imprint on my practice and understanding. With this comes a deep sense of responsibility — to honor, preserve, and carry forward the living tradition they have entrusted to me.

Words fall short in expressing my gratitude to my Shifu, Grandmaster Chen Zhenglei (陳正雷) — one of China's "Top Ten Martial Arts Masters," an 11th-generation successor of Chen Family Tai Chi. Under his tutelage, I proudly became a 12th-generation lineage holder, entrusted with the preservation and transmission of Chen-style Tai Chi's traditional methods.

It was also a tremendous honor to have Professor Yu Dinghai (虞定海) as my doctoral advisor at Shanghai University of Sport. A highly respected expert and holder of the distinguished nine-duan rank in both Tai Chi and Qigong, Professor Yu's mentorship has been pivotal in shaping both my academic and martial arts paths.

In addition to these luminaries, this book has been enriched by the insights and inspiration I have drawn from other remarkable masters and grandmasters, including:

Chen Xiaowang (陳小旺), Zhu Tiancai (朱天才), Wu Bin (吳斌), Abraham Liu, Dan Lee, Zang Hongxian (臧洪先), Liu Jishun (劉積順), Su Zifang (蘇自芳), Chen Sitan (陳斯坦), Xie Yelei (謝業雷), and Kong Xiangdong (孔祥東).

I am deeply committed to honoring their teachings and advancing the spirit of Tai Chi they so generously shared. Any imperfections in my interpretations are entirely my own.

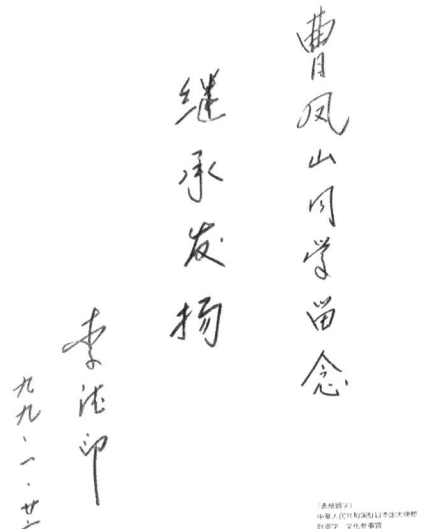

李天驥 (1915—1996) 李家第二代武術人，自幼隨父習武 1930 年到山東國術館深造，畢業后留館任教。 不久調任陵縣國術館館長，獲山東國術館長測驗賽第一名。1938 年隨父親到東北地區創建太極拳研究社。1954 年李天驥奉調入京，任中央體育學院武術班教練組長。 1955 年參加「簡化太極拳」創編。 這是新中國第一套國家編定的太極拳教材，為初學者入門和太極拳普及提供了方便。 李天驥是24式簡化太極拳的執筆者、示範者。 1959 年日本友人松村先生率團來華訪問，周總理向客人介紹了太極拳運動，李天驥受命向日本客人傳授簡化太極拳。此後，日本掀起太極拳熱潮，他先後六次赴日本講學訪問，被日本武術界稱為"太極拳之父"

In 1954, Li Tianji was appointed head coach of the martial arts program at the Central Sports Institute. In 1955, he was the primary author and demonstrator of the Simplified Tai Chi Form 24.

繼承發揚

Inherit and Carry Forward

Introduction

Over the past fifty years of teaching Tai Chi, I have consistently observed a common challenge among students: the transition from bare-hand forms to weapon forms. Tai Chi weapon routines often differ significantly from their bare-hand counterparts, requiring students to learn entirely new postures and memorize unfamiliar sequences. This disconnect between bare-hand and weapon training can make the learning process feel overwhelming and inefficient.

To address this issue, I embarked on an experiment to enhance teaching effectiveness by using a familiar bare-hand form as the structural template for weapon routines. My goal was to design weapon forms that students could learn quickly and remember easily—each one rooted in the same foundational sequence.

By preserving the structure and posture names of the original bare-hand form, students are able to focus on refining their internal skills rather than struggling to learn entirely new movements. At the same time, each weapon brings its own unique "flavor" to the form—much like grafting different fruits onto the same tree. These variations cultivate different qualities, such as spiral energy (silk reeling), structural alignment and connectivity, and integrated whole-body strength.

This approach led to the development of a series of weapon routines based on the Simplified Tai Chi Form 24 for Tai Chi Healthways' instructor training curriculum. Over the past fifteen years, I have published four instructional DVDs/videos demonstrating these adaptations:

- Tai Chi Double Bang in Form 24
- Tai Chi Cane in Form 24
- Tai Chi Ball in Form 24
- Tai Chi Long Staff in Form 24

(visit https://taichihealthways.com/all-dvds/).

This method not only simplifies the learning process but also highlights the inherent versatility of Tai Chi as a unified system. By using a bare-hand form as a foundational template, students can train the body's energy flow and inner strength in a consistent framework. In this way, any Tai Chi form or style can serve as a bridge between bare-hand and weapon practice, allowing for seamless integration and deeper exploration of the art's internal mechanics.

Why Tai Chi Form 24?

The Simplified Tai Chi Form 24, often shortened to Tai Chi Form 24, is most widely practiced in China and worldwide. Its popularity lies in its accessibility, making it an excellent starting point for beginners while preserving the health benefits and traditional essence of Tai Chi. This form's concise structure, consisting of 24 movements, provides a solid foundation for adapting to weapon training.

I was first introduced to Tai Chi Form 24 in 1978 when I began my college life at Beijing Renmin University. Under the guidance of Professor Li Deyin (李德印), the head coach of my college Wushu team, I learned this form as a required routine. Before that, I had practiced Tai Chi in my hometown of Penglai, China, the traditional Northern Wu style Tai Chi passed down through Wang Maozhai - Liu Guangdou - Liu Wancang (王茂齋-劉光鬥-劉晚蒼). My ten years of life in Beijing allowed me to explore various Tai Chi styles, including Chen, Yang, Wu, and Sun, as well as numerous standard and competition forms. These experiences deepened my understanding of Tai Chi's roots, which ultimately trace back to the Chen family old frame. This realization led me to become a disciple of Chen Zhenglei (陈正雷), and I became the 12th-generation lineage holder of Chen family Tai Chi.

The creation of Tai Chi Form 24 dates back to seventy years ago, when the Chinese State Physical Culture and Sports Committee initiated a project to simplify traditional Tai Chi for mass participation. Tai Chi experts such as Wu Tunan (吳圖南), Chen Fake (陳發科), Gao Ruizhou (高瑞周), Tian Zhenfeng (田鎮峰), Li Tianji (李天驥), and Tang Hao (唐豪) collaborated to create an accessible form based on the representative movements of major Tai Chi styles. While the original draft was deemed too complex, a revised version using movements from the popular Yang style was finalized by Mao Bohao (毛伯浩), Li Tianji (李天驥), Tang hao (唐豪), and Wu Gaoming (吳高明) in 1955. This version emphasized health benefits and ease of learning, which contributed to its widespread adoption. However, over time, the form's original purpose as a health-oriented practice was sometimes overshadowed by its use in sport competitions.

In this book, first I provide illustrations of the complete bare-hand Tai Chi Form 24 as the core routine providing foundational movements, postures, and principles that serve as a basis for adapting to weapon routines. There are a number of pictures presented for each posture with arrow lines that clearly show the path the arms and legs took. The illustrations uniquely emphasize Tai Chi's core philosophy of Yin and Yang harmony by focusing on the close and open patterns within the movements.

In addition to detailed instructions, I am offering layered insights into each Tai Chi posture from three integrated perspectives: 1) Wellness / Self-Healing – focusing on internal energy cultivation, meridian stimulation, organ support, and releasing stagnation. 2) Fitness / Body Conditioning – emphasizing spring-like qualities such as elasticity, compressibility, twistability, and structural integrity. 3) Martial Arts Application – interpreting how each posture embodies practical techniques like redirecting force, uprooting, joint control, or striking. This framework not only honors the depth of Tai Chi but also makes it accessible and meaningful to practitioners from various backgrounds. These annotations will support your journey toward mastering Tai Chi Form 24, deepening your understanding and connection to its profound principles.

Tai Chi's wellness function is particularly associated with the TCM meridian system and the harmony of Yin and Yang energy. The body has twelve primary meridian channels, with six connecting the internal organs to the hands and six linking them to the feet. Additionally, the Conception Vessel (Ren Mai) runs along the center front of the torso, while the Governor Vessel (Du Mai) flows along the spine on the back, working together to balance and regulate the body's Yin and Yang energy flow.

In TCM, each of the twelve primary organs' meridian is associated with two powerful energetic points: a Mu (募穴) point on the front of the body, known as an "energy-gathering" point, and a Shu (腧穴) point on the back, referred to as an "energy-releasing" point. Together, these form a dynamic gateway system that regulates the flow of qi (vital energy) through the body.

In the Daoist's view, the Mu point is soft, receptive, and nourishing, not only for the meridian's qi of the organ gathers, but also considered as energetic "doors" through which universal Qi can enter to support and replenish the internal organ. The Shu point is more active and expressive, and serves as a release valve for tension, stagnation, excess heat, or emotional stress to disperse like smoke rising into the air.

In Tai Chi practice, this concept is embodied through the coordinated opening and closing of movements linked with mindful breathing to form a natural rhythm: inhale to receive through the Mu points, exhale to release through the Shu points. As you close in your arms, visualize to hug in fresh Qi entering through the Mu points; as you open arms, imagine releasing toxins through the Shu points. This creates a fluid, balanced energy flow that mirrors the harmony of Yin and Yang.

Each Tai Chi posture is intricately designed to stimulate one of two specific primary meridian pathways and a few secondary pathways, promoting energy circulation and internal organ health. The coordinated movements of the hands and feet activate these energy channels, enhancing the function of corresponding organs. By integrating breath and intention in movement, Tai Chi serves as a powerful tool for holistic healing, fostering internal balance, vitality, and overall well-being.

Tai Chi's fitness benefits are exemplified through the development of your body's spring-like qualities to enhance your balance, flexibility, strength, core stability, and overall physical vitality. Elasticity represents the ability of your body's dynamic stretching and unstretching much like a spring, maintaining a supple and responsive body. It is mainly applied on your torso and arms elongation and contraction to store and release energy with ease. Twistability highlights the rotational and spiraling movements central to Tai Chi. This principle emphasizes your body's ability to coil and uncoil, creating spinning and internal torque that generates centrifugal power and flow. It often involves your waist, spine, and limbs working in harmony. Compressibility represents your body's ability to condense energy inward, much like compressing a spring, before releasing it outward. It is capable of absorbing incoming force and rebounding it outward without stiffness or rigidity. It is mainly applied on your hips and sink to heels to connect with earth energy, ready to expand when needed.

Tai Chi's martial function can be distilled into a seamless flow from defense to offense, achieved through the strategic application of eight action energies combined with five methods of footwork. The four primary energies—Peng (ward-off), Lu (roll-back), Ji (press), and An (push)—establish the foundation of Tai Chi's defensive and offensive structure. These are complemented by the four secondary energies—Cai (pluck), Lie (split), Zhou (elbow strike), and Kao (torso bump)—which refine counterattacks. At its core, Tai Chi defense begins with ward-off and roll-back, neutralizing incoming force while maintaining balance, then striking your opponent off balance. This dynamic interplay of yielding and issuing force embodies the essence of Tai Chi martial art practice.

The main body of this book is to introduce three illustrated routines of Tai Chi Form 24 application with different weapons. It provides a practical and innovative strategy for extending the health benefits and principles of Tai Chi into weapon training. By using a universally practiced form as the template, students and instructors can efficiently learn and teach multiple weapon routines without being overwhelmed by new forms.

The Tai Chi Double Clubbell (or double-bang) in Form 24 is a practice I developed to address modern health concerns, such as carpal tunnel syndrome and finger arthritis. This form is particularly beneficial for individuals with Parkinson's disease, as holding objects in hand practicing Tai Chi helps stabilize tremors. Each posture incorporates small wrist circles driven by the silk-reeling energy flow, which stimulates the six hand meridian primary (or original 原穴) energy points near the wrist. This practice not only improves wrist flexibility but also helps prevent heart and lung problems by enhancing energy circulation. These six primary energy points are associated with the prenatal qi of six internal organs. They act as "switches" to regulate organ function and ensure that postnatal qi, which is derived from food and air, is being effectively used to support the body's needs. If an organ is weak, stimulating its primary point helps it access the prenatal qi more efficiently. For example, Shen-men (HT 7 神門) on the wrist is used to calm the mind and treat heart-related conditions like palpitations and anxiety. Additionally, double clubbell weight can train your muscles and strength, and also lays a foundation for two-hand coordination and advanced double-weapon forms.

The Tai Chi Cane in Form 24 is a versatile tool designed for self-defense and as a foundation for practicing sword or broadsword forms. In daily life, a walking cane is often seen as a mobility aid, but its innocuous appearance belies its potential as a weapon. Its upward-sweeping parries and non-threatening stance make it an ideal tool for modern self-defense, especially in environments where traditional weapons are restricted. This form equips practitioners with practical weapon techniques while preserving the health benefits of Tai Chi.

Tai Chi Staff in Form 24 using a long staff is an essential training tool for developing internal power (內勁). Striking with the staff generates vibrations that resonate through the body, enhancing structural alignment, balance, and coordination. This practice provides a solid foundation for training in long-handled weapons, such as the spear or halberd, and strengthens the connection between the practitioner's inner energy and their external movements.

Whether you are an instructor seeking to enrich your curriculum or an experienced student looking to deepen your practice, this book serves as a guide to integrating Tai Chi's bare-hand and weapon routines into a cohesive system. With clear illustrations, philosophical insights, and practical applications, this book bridges the gap between tradition and modernity, offering a path to both mastery and self-discovery. Professor Li Deyin praised: "Your concept and creation effectively balance tradition, innovation, safety, and convenience, reflecting the spirit of maintaining authenticity while embracing innovation" (你的構思和創編很好解決了傳統，新穎，安全，方便的矛盾，體現了守正創新的精神).

蛇身下勢

Snake creeping down

Part I
Illustrated Simplified Tai Chi Form 24

To help readers understand the directions of the postures, directional references have been established as follows: when the figure faces the reader, it is considered facing south; when the back is toward the reader, it is facing north; when the figure's face is turned toward the reader's right side, it is facing east; and when turned to the left side, it is facing west. The solid and dotted arrows in the illustrations indicate the paths of hand and foot movements to be executed. Solid lines indicate the movement direction of the right hand and foot, while dotted lines represent the directional tendencies of the left hand and foot.

Posture 1: Opening Form

Photo 1-1   Photo 1-2

Movement 1:

Stand facing the south and step your left foot sideways so that your feet are shoulder-width apart, ensuring your toes point relatively straight forward. Allow your arms to hang naturally by your sides, relaxed but ready. Keep your gaze directed forward, maintaining focus and awareness of your surroundings. This stance forms a stable and neutral foundation, ideal for beginning movements or transitioning into action (Photo 1-1).

Note: The directional lines and vectors illustrated in Photo 1 delineate the movement trajectories depicted in the succeeding image, elaborated upon in the subsequent textual paragraph. This descriptive methodology persists throughout the remaining illustrations.

Movement 2:

Raise your arms forward and upward until they reach shoulder height, keeping them naturally extended and relaxed. Palms face downward, with your fingers gently aligned and pointing forward. Avoid locking your elbows to maintain a sense of fluidity and readiness (Photo 1-2).

Photo 1-3

Movement 3:

Sink your hips toward your heels and bend your knees slightly, grounding yourself in a stable stance by keeping 60% weight on heels of your feet, and 40% on the balls and toes. Imagine your heel as the taproot and toes are lateral roots of a big tree. This body weight distribution will prevent your knees from strains and develop your leg muscles and strength, as well as improve your balance. At the same time, lower your elbows and gently press your palms downward to about hip height. Relax your shoulders and let your posture convey calmness and stability, preparing for the next movement (Photo 1-3).

Insights: Unlike ordinary physical exercise, Tai Chi avoids stiff or forceful movement. The Opening Form helps you to relax, center yourself, and gently activate the meridians to promote smooth inner energy flow. This move is a fundamental exercise in Tai Chi for developing the body's spring-like qualities in hips compressibility. It trains your body's ability to condense like compressing a spring, before releasing it. It conveys the idea of connecting with the earth and storing potential energy while staying calm and grounded, ready to expand with ease.

Posture 2: Part Wild Horse's Mane

Photo 2-1   Photo 2-2

Movement 1:

Raise your right palm upward in a curved motion from your right side while simultaneously moving your left palm downward in a smooth, flowing arc. Your hands trace a counterclockwise circular pattern, creating a sense of harmony and balance. Continue the movement until your right forearm rests naturally in front of your upper chest and your left palm aligns near your lower belly. At the end of the motion, both palms should face each other, as if gently holding an invisible ball. Shift your left foot slightly inward, allowing only the toes to lightly touch the floor for stability and readiness. This final position represents a closing and guarding stance, with your hands poised to protect your centerline while keeping your body grounded and centered (Photo 2-1).

Movement 2:

Turn your body to the left and step your left foot outward to the east. Shift your weight onto your left foot and bend your left knee to form a bow stance. Simultaneously, raise your left palm to face height with the palm angled slightly upward and the elbow slightly bent. Lower your right palm to the side of your right hip, with the palm facing downward and fingers pointing forward (Photo 2-2).

Photo 2-3 Photo 2-4

Movement 3:

Shift your weight back, raise your left toes, and turn them outward before placing your entire foot on the floor. Next, turn your body to the left and bring your right foot next to your left. At the same time, form a hold-ball gesture in front of your left chest, with your left hand on top (Photo 2-3).

Movement 4:

Turn your body to the right slightly and step your right foot forward to the east and shift your weight onto your right foot and bend your right knee to form a bow stance. Simultaneously, raise your right palm to face height with the palm angled slightly upward and the elbow slightly bent. Lower your left palm to the side of your left hip, with the palm facing downward and fingers pointing forward. Keep your gaze focused on your right hand (Photo 2-4).

Photo 2-5   Photo 2-6

Movement 5:

Repeat Movement 3 and 4 reversing "left" and "right" (Photo 2-5 and 2-6).

Insights: *Parting the Wild Horse's Mane* expresses the yin-yang dynamic at the heart of Tai Chi—through coordinated opening and closing. The movement begins with the palms "holding the ball," as if embracing fresh, vital energy from nature. This imagery helps draw energy inward through the Mu points at the front of the torso, which are associated with gathering and nourishing qi. As the arms open, you can visualize releasing stress and stagnation through the back Shu points and the three hand-Yin channels that run from the chest down the inner arms to the fingers. This action promotes internal cleansing and energy flow, especially good for the heart and lungs. Physically, the movement stretches and twists the body in a spiral, enhancing flexibility, elasticity, and coordination. The controlled expansion and contraction condition the fascia and joints, developing a supple yet resilient structure. The waist and spine serve as the axis of movement, generating internal torque that links the upper and lower body. In martial terms, this posture typically trains the shoulder bump energy. It starts with ward-off arms protecting the centerline, smoothly transitions into roll-back to absorb and neutralize force, and then step in and insert the shoulder under the opponent's armpit to counter with precise back shoulder strike with grounded power. It's a seamless blend of softness and strength. The step to close in is very important to use the shoulder strike. Additionally, *Parting the Wild Horse's Mane* normally consists of three linked steps forward, and can be effectively used with splitting energy to escape out a group of attackers.

Part I: Illustrated Simplified Tai Chi Form 24

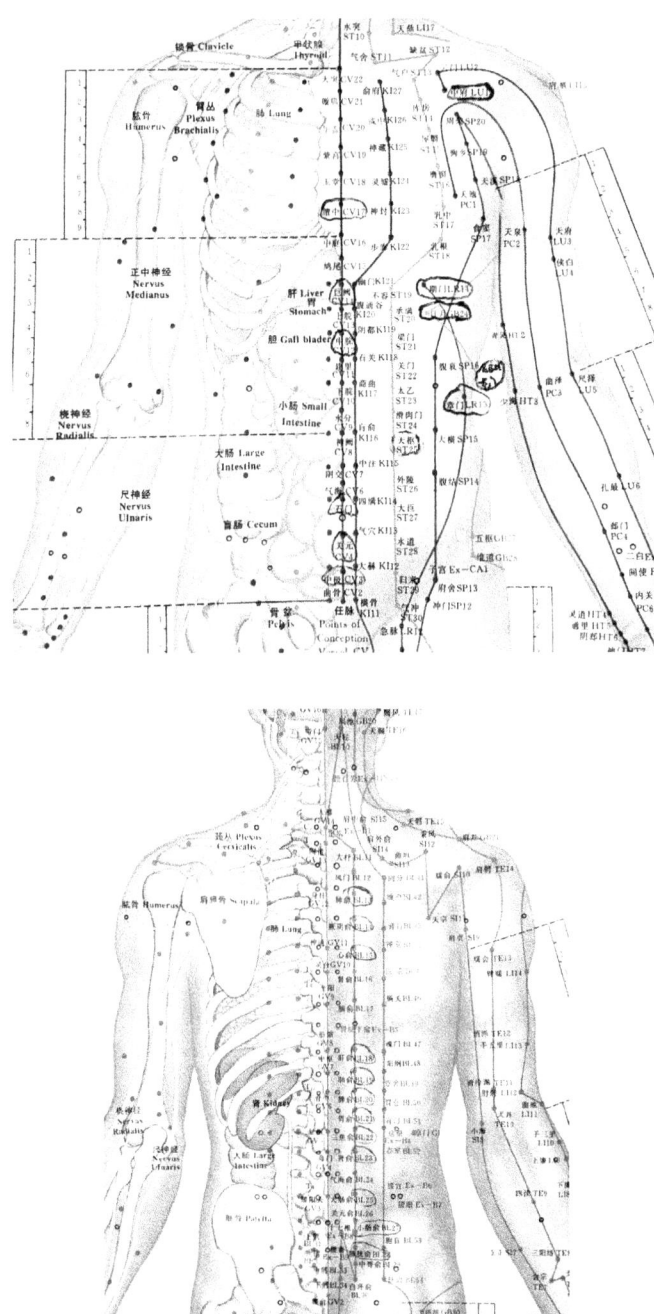

Picture of Mu gathering points and Shu releasing points

Note: In TCM, each internal organ has an energy gathering point (募穴), a place where qi and blood of the corresponding organ gather and concentrate in the body. While it primarily gathers internal energy, it also serves as a bridge between the body and the external environment. In Qigong and Daoist practices, certain energy points are thought to be more sensitive to external qi and act as gateways for absorbing energy from nature. For example, the upper abdomen (CV12中脘), located near the solar plexus, is a known energy absorption center in many traditions. The chest center (CV17膻中), and the lower dantian (CV4關元) are particularly associated with this function. Those energy gathering points are all located in front of your torso.

Posture 3: White Crane Spreading Its Wings

Photo 3-1   Photo 3-2

Movement 1:

Step your right foot half a step closer to your left foot while slightly turning your torso to the left. Form a hold-ball gesture in front of your left chest, with your left hand on top, with your weight mainly on the left foot. This position serves as a closing pose, protecting your front centerline and training your compressibility on your left hip to store energy for the expansion in the next move (Photo 3-1).

Movement 2:

Shift your weight back to your right leg, and move your left foot slightly forward, placing only the toes on the floor to form a left empty stance. Simultaneously, raise your right hand to the front of your forehead and lower your left hand to the side of your left hip in curved paths, keeping both arms rounded. You are relatively facing the east (Photo 3-2).

Insights: *White Crane Spreading Its Wings* reflects the harmony of wellness, fitness, and martial arts in Tai Chi. As the arms close and the hips sink, the body stores energy—drawing fresh qi through the Mu points at the front of the torso. Opening the arms then releases tension via the back Shu points and the hand-Yin channels, especially supporting energy flow and benefiting the spleen and stomach meridians. These channels connect the torso from foot to rib (spleen) and from face to foot (stomach), aiding digestion and grounding. The posture also trains elasticity in the torso and arms, while cultivating waist flexibility through gentle spiraling. In martial terms, this movement embodies both defense and offense in a single, elegant gesture. The inward movement of arms protects the centerline. As the arms expand outward, they deflect incoming force with one arm, and the other strikes, mimicking a crane slicing the air with its wings to ward off attackers. The technique allows for simultaneous high and low targeting: the fingers of the right hand can threaten or strike toward the opponent's eyes, while the left hand delivers a low blow—such as to the groin—disrupting balance and intent with a swift counterattack.

Posture 4: Brush Knee on Both Sides

Photo 4-1   Photo 4-2

Movement 1:

Move your right palm in a downward arc, guided by the twisting of your torso, from the front of your forehead to the side of your right hip. Simultaneously, move your left palm in an inward arc from the side of your left hip to the front of your chest. At the same time, draw your left foot closer to your right foot, forming a closed defensive pose (Photo 4-1).

Movement 2:

Step forward with your left foot to the east into a left bow stance. Simultaneously, circle your right palm upward from the rear right corner, above your right shoulder, and push it forward to the east at nose height. Sink your right shoulder and keep your right elbow slightly down while pushing your right palm. At the same time, brush your left palm in an arc through your centerline to the side of your left hip. This movement creates a "brush away and push out" open pose (Photo 4-2).

Photo 4-3   Photo 4-4

Movement 3:

Shift your weight slightly to raise the toes of your left foot, turning your torso a bit to the left. Then, move up your right foot to the side of your left foot with the ball touching the floor. At the same time, roll your right palm back toward your front to protect your centerline, while moving your left palm in a parrying motion to the back side of your left hip (Photo 4-3).

Movement 4:

Brush your right palm downward in a curved path along your centerline to the outside of your right knee. Simultaneously, step your right foot forward to the east into a right bow stance. At the same time, circle your left palm upward in an inward arc from the side of your left hip to the side of your left ear, then push it forward to the east in front of your chest, with the fingers of your right palm aligned at nose height. Sink your left shoulder and keep your left elbow slightly down while pushing your left palm (Photo 4-4.

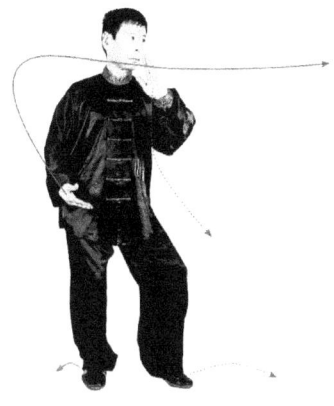 

Photo 4-5 Photo 4-6

Movement 5:

Repeat Movement 3 and 4 reversing "left" and "right" (Photo 4-5 and 4-6).

Insights: *Brush Knee on Both Sides* offers integrated benefits across energy flow, flexibility, and martial function. This posture helps smooth and activate the Bladder Meridian—the body's longest channel—running along the spine and the backs of the legs. It supports fluid metabolism and the circulation of internal fluids. The forward push in the movement aids in releasing stagnation through the back Shu points, promoting internal clarity and ease. At the end of the push, when the hand returns toward the torso, it can be used as gathering natural energy to the Mu points for nourishment. Physically, the posture trains coordinated twisting of the torso while extending the legs, spine, and arms, enhancing whole-body flexibility and elasticity. In martial practice, one hand deflects incoming force with a parry and brush, while the other delivers a precise forward strike—combining defense and offense in a single flowing motion.

Posture 5: Playing a Guitar

Photo 5-1   Photo 5-2

Movement 1:

Step your right foot half a step closer to your left heel. Simultaneously, withdraw your right palm halfway toward the center of your chest in a slightly downward and inward path, while raising your left palm from the side of your left hip in an inward curve to meet the front of your right hand. The fingers of your right hand should reach shoulder height and in front of the left hand. This posture is regarded as a closing and protective pose (Photo 5-1).

Movement 2:

Step your left foot forward half a step to the east, placing the heel on the floor and toes up with the knee slightly bent to form a left empty stance. At the same time, bring your right palm toward the left elbow with the palm facing left, and extend your left palm forward and upward to nose height with the palm facing right and the elbow slightly bent. Sink both hips, lengthen the spine, and lift the head, keeping the shoulders and elbows relaxed and down (Photo 5-2).

Insights: *Playing a Guitar* is a classic Tai Chi posture for absorbing energy through the Mu points at the front of the torso. With the chest and lower abdomen slightly concave, the body forms a gentle suction that draws in qi from nature. Sinking the hips builds compressibility and spring-like power in the lower body. This posture not only fosters stillness and centeredness but also conditions the body to store and release energy efficiently. In martial application, both hands work in unison to guard the chest, ideally containing the opponent's hand and elbow in a joint-locking structure—blending defense, control, and subtle power.

Posture 6: Repulse Monkey

Photo 6-1

Photo 6-2

Movement 1:

Turn your torso slightly to the right, moving your right palm in a downward curve past your abdomen and then upward to shoulder height, with the right arm opening backward and outward. Simultaneously, extend your left palm forward slightly, parrying it gently to the left. At the end of the motion, both arms should be wide open, with elbows slightly bent and palms facing upward. First, glance at your right hand while it is going back, then shift your gaze to your left hand in front of you (Photo 6-1).

Movement 2:

Step your left foot back, resting it momentarily near your right foot with the ball of the foot touching the floor. If your balance is steady, you may hold your left foot in the air without touching the ground. Simultaneously, bend your right arm and draw your right palm past your right ear before pushing it forward in front of your chest, while your left hand moves in a downward curve toward your left abdomen. Ensure your right palm does not fully extend in the push. Your body should form a contracting and controlling posture (Photo 6-2).

Photo 6-3   Photo 6-4

Movement 3:

Step your left foot back to the west and turn your torso to the left. Shift your weight onto your left foot to form a right empty stance, adjusting your right heel outward to open your hips so the toes point forward, avoiding strain on your right knee. Simultaneously, move your left palm in a downward curve past the outside of your left hip before raising it to shoulder height. Extend your right palm forward to the east, forming an open-arms posture with both elbows slightly bent and palms facing upward. First, glance at your left hand as it moves back, then shift your gaze to your right hand in front of you (Photo 6-3).

Movement 4:

Step your right foot back, resting it momentarily near your left foot with the ball of the foot touching the floor. If your balance is steady, you may hold your right foot in the air without touching the ground. Simultaneously, bend your left arm and draw your left palm past your left ear before pushing it forward in front of your chest, while your right hand moves in a downward curve toward your right abdomen. Ensure your left palm does not fully extend in the push. Your body should form a contracting and controlling posture (Photo 6-4).

Photo 6-5　　　　　　　　　　Photo 6-6

Movement 5:

Step back your right foot and repeat Movement 1 and 2 (Photo 6-5 and 6-6).

Photo 6-7　　　　　　　　　　Photo 6-8

Movement 6:

Repeat Movement 3 and 4 (Photo 6-7 and 6-8).

Photo 6-9

Movement 7:

Step back your right foot, and repeat Movement 1 (Photo 6-9).

Insights: *Repulse Monkey* offers a dynamic self-massage for the back's meridian channels, enhancing qi circulation and releasing tension along the spine. The see-saw motion gently stretches the back and stimulates the twelve Shu points on either side of the spine—key gateways for releasing stagnation and regulating internal energy. It flushes the bladder meridians through the counterbalanced crossing stretches of the back leg with the front pushing arm and the front leg with the back drawing arm. As the torso twists left and right, the arms alternately extend and retract, building elasticity and rotational strength in the spine and shoulders. In martial terms, the movement combines yielding and redirecting with timely counter-strikes, making it both graceful and tactically effective. It is called "Use retreat as bait; within the retreat lies an attack." (以退為誘餌，退裡有攻).

Posture 7: Grasp the Bird's Tail - Left

Photo 7-1   Photo 7-2

Movement 1:

Withdraw your left foot toward your right foot, with the ball of your left foot lightly touching the floor to form a left empty stance. Simultaneously, draw your right palm inward to the front of your chest, passing by your right shoulder, while your left palm moves in a downward curve in front of your belly. Both palms face each other, forming a hold-ball posture. This represents a closing defensive pose (Photo 7-1).

Movement 2:

Step your left foot forward to the east, bending the knee into a left bow stance. Simultaneously, roll-back your right hand in a downward curve to the side of your right hip, while positioning your left forearm and the back of your left hand in front of your chest, as if warding off an incoming force. Keep both arms rounded, ensuring the movement and separation of the palms are coordinated (Photo 7-2).

Photo 7-3   Photo 7-4

Movement 3:

Turn your torso slightly to the left as you extend your left hand forward to the east, with the palm turning downward, and bring your right hand upward beneath your left forearm, with the palm turning upward. Although it appears as a brief pause, continue fluidly by turning your torso slightly to the right while pulling both hands downward in a curved motion, as if gripping an opponent's elbow and wrist to pull them down toward your right hip side. As you do this, shift your weight onto your back foot (Photo 7-3).

Movement 4:

Continue the circular motion of your arms, allowing your right hand to extend back and sideways at shoulder height while your left hand bends in front of your chest with the palm facing inward. Gradually turn your torso slightly to the left, aligning yourself to face east, while bend your right arm at the elbow, bringing your right hand to rest just inside your left wrist. As you do this, shift your weight slowly onto your left leg, transitioning into a left bow stance. Maintain a rounded shape with both arms and press both hands forward toward the east in a controlled and harmonious motion. Keep your gaze directed toward the east, embodying focus and intent of pressing (Photo 7-4).

Photo 7-5　　　　　　　　　　Photo 7-6

Movement 5:

Turn both palms downward, extending them forward slightly and separating them to shoulder width apart. Gradually shift your weight back onto your right leg, drawing both hands back in a smooth downward curve to the front of your abdomen, with the palms angled obliquely downward. This motion mimics controlling or redirecting an opponent's arms or hands, forming a protective and grounded pose. You may lift the toes of your left foot slightly off the floor, facilitating the weight shift to your back leg. Maintain a relaxed but focused posture, ensuring your movements are deliberate and coordinated (Photo 7-5).

Movement 6:

6. Gradually transfer your weight onto your left leg, transitioning into a stable left bow stance. Simultaneously, push both palms forward in a smooth upward curve until your wrists reach shoulder height, with the palms facing forward. Maintain a steady and flowing motion, keeping your arms slightly bent at elbows and relaxed. Direct your gaze straight ahead to the east, projecting focus and intent while maintaining balance and stability in your stance (Photo 7-6).

Insights: *Grasp the Bird's Tail* is a hallmark of Yang-style Tai Chi, weaving together energy flow, structural training, and martial skill. Through three coordinated weight shifts forward and back, it promotes smooth energy circulation—dispersing stagnation and drawing in fresh qi from nature. The movement channels energy downward through the foot-Yang meridians on the outer side of legs, rebounds earth energy upward via the foot-Yin meridians on the inner side of legs, and transmits it through the torso to the arms and hands. It's a complete training for the body's spring-like qualities: twistability, compressibility, and elasticity. The roll-back relies on rotational power from the waist, while the press and push are rooted in the hips, sinking and compressing action. In martial terms, this sequence neutralizes incoming force, uproots the opponent, and counteracts with grounded, expansive power of press and push.

Posture 8: Grasp the Bird's Tail - Right

Photo 8-1

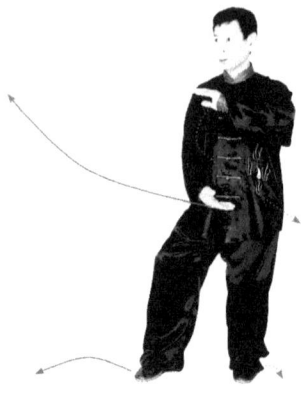

Photo 8-2

Movement 1:

Shift your weight onto your right leg as you gently turn your torso to the right. At the same time, sweep your right arm in a smooth, horizontal arc, slightly upward, toward the west as if deflecting an incoming force. Simultaneously, pivot your left foot, turning the toes inward to face south, aligning your stance with stability and control. Keep your left palm open and extended, maintaining warding-off toward the east, Focus on coordinating your torso and arm movements fluidly while grounding your stance (Photo 8-1).

Movement 2:

Shift your weight onto your left foot and bring your right foot beside your left, with the toes and ball of your right foot lightly touching the floor to form a right empty stance. Simultaneously, guide your right hand in a smooth downward curve toward your abdomen, while your left hand moves inward to the front of your upper chest. Together, the hands form a rounded hold-ball posture, with the left hand positioned on top and the right hand below, palms facing each other. This posture symbolizes a closing defensive stance, embodying readiness and control, while maintaining balance and focus (Photo 8-2).

Photo 8-3

Photo 8-4

Photo 8-5

Photo 8-6

Photo 8-7

Movement 3:

Repeat the Movement 2, 3, 4, 5, and 6 in the previous posture Grasp the Bird's Tail - Left, and reversing "left" and "right" (Photo 8-3, 8-4, 8-5, 8-6, and 8-7).

Insights: Same as Posture 7.

Posture 9: Single Whip

Photo 9-1

Photo 9-2

Movement 1:

Sink your right hip and shift your weight back onto your left foot while turning your right toes inward to align with your stance. At the same time, rotate your torso to the left, smoothly carrying your hands leftward—your left palm tracing an upward arc past your face, while your right palm follows a downward curve near your belly. Then, shift your weight onto your right foot as you draw your left foot beside your right, keeping your movements fluid and controlled. As your weight transitions, allow your arms to continue their circular motion from your left to the right, guiding your left palm downward to rest in front of your right ribs. Simultaneously, your right palm arcs upward past your face toward the right front corner, then turns outward as your fingertips bunch together and your wrist bends into a hook hand. Maintain a sense of balance and energy flow throughout the movement, ensuring each transition is seamless and connected (Photo 9-1).

Movement 2:

Guide your left palm in a smooth upward curve to the front of your right shoulder, maintaining a soft, rounded structure. As you turn your torso to the left, let your left palm naturally rise to ward off in front of your face, creating a protective barrier. Following this leftward motion, execute a controlled parry and whip with your left palm, directing it toward the east. Simultaneously, step your left foot forward into a strong and balanced left bow stance. At the final position, your left palm is extended with the elbow slightly bent and fingertips at eye level, facing east with intent, while your right hook hand remains extended toward the southwest corner, maintaining a counterbalance and structural integrity within the form (Photo 9-2).

Insights: *Single Whip* is one of the most expansive postures in Tai Chi, designed to open the torso and release deep-seated stress and stagnation. The wide, horizontal whipping motion creates a centrifugal force that particularly helps refresh and circulate energy in the heart and lungs. This form also symbolizes the harmony between heaven and earth—Yang and Yin—with the left fingers reaching upward and the right fingers pointing downward. The back leg and front arm form an open extension structure, and the front leg bent at the knee with the back hooked hand form a closure foundation to hold energy balance. It's also a key posture for developing spring-like qualities in the body, especially elasticity and twistability. In martial application, the right hook hand deflects or controls incoming force, while the left hand delivers a sharp, whipping counterstrike.

Posture 10: Wave Hands Like Clouds

Photo 10-1

Photo 10-2

Movement 1:

Sink your left hip and gently draw your right heel inward, and shift your weight gradually onto your right foot while simultaneously turning your torso to the right in a controlled, fluid motion. As your body rotates, guide your left palm downward in a gentle curve toward the front of your belly, maintaining a relaxed yet intentional posture. At the same time, turn your left foot inward so that your toes face relatively south, ensuring a stable stance. Release the tension in your right hook hand, allowing it to open naturally with the palm facing forward toward your right front (Photo 10-1).

Movement 2:

Guide your right palm downward in a smooth, flowing curve toward the front of your belly, maintaining a gentle yet controlled motion. Simultaneously, lift your left palm in an upward arc, bringing it to the front of your right shoulder while keeping your arm rounded and relaxed. As you turn your torso to the left, shift your weight onto your left foot and bring your right foot in, placing it beside your left foot for a moment of centered stability. Meanwhile, as your torso continues its turn, let your left palm glide past the front of your face, gradually rotating outward until it faces your left front. Maintain a sense of fluidity and mindfulness, ensuring your movements are both connected and harmonious (Photo 10-2).

Part I: Illustrated Simplified Tai Chi Form 24

Photo 10-3

Photo 10-4

Movement 3:

Sweep your right hand in a smooth, upward curve toward the front of your left shoulder, maintaining the arm rounded. Allow the movement to flow continuously past your face, guiding your hand to the right side while gradually turning your palm outward. As this unfolds, shift your weight onto your right foot and rotate your torso toward the right front corner, ensuring a controlled and balanced transition. Simultaneously, lower your left palm in a gentle downward arc toward the front of your belly, keeping your arm relaxed yet engaged. As your weight shifts, step your left foot out to the east with intention, creating a stable foundation for the next movement. Maintain a sense of harmony between the upper and lower hands, allowing energy to flow seamlessly through the posture (Photo 10-3).

Movement 4:

Repeat Movement 2 (Photo 10-4).

Photo 10-5

Photo 10-6

Movement 5:

Repeat Movement 3 and 4 (Photo 10-5, 10-6).

Insights: *Wave Hands Like Clouds* is a classic Tai Chi posture that promotes smooth energy circulation, particularly benefiting the heart and lungs. It draws in fresh qi through the front torso's Mu points and releases stagnation through the back Shu points. This movement also activates the Belt Vessel (带脉)—one of the Eight Extraordinary Meridians (奇经八脉)—which encircles the waist horizontally and stabilizes the lower back and abdomen. By keeping this vessel active, the posture helps regulate those six vertical foot-meridians passing through it, preventing energy blockage and promoting balance. The continuous twisting of the waist enhances torso flexibility and supports the reduction of fat accumulation around the midsection. In martial application, this posture excels in neutralizing attacks through soft, lateral parrying. Its flowing motion redirects force with ease and sets up counterstrikes using plucking or splitting energy, demonstrating Tai Chi's principle of using softness to overcome hardness.

Posture 11: Single Whip

Photo 11-1   Photo 11-2

Movement 1:

Ward off with your right hand by sweeping it in an upward curve from the front of your belly to the front of your left shoulder, creating a protective and expansive motion. Simultaneously, lower your left hand to guard near the front of your left hip, maintaining a balanced and defensive posture. Shift your weight onto your right foot while turning your torso slightly to the right. As you do this, guide your right palm in a smooth roll-back motion toward the front of your right shoulder, gradually turning the palm into a hook hand, with fingertips bunching together and the wrist slightly bent. At the same time, parry your left palm inward to align with the front of your right ribs, ensuring a compact and protective stance. Lift your left heel lightly off the ground, keeping your toes touching the floor, positioning yourself in a poised, ready-to-step-out left empty stance (Photo 11-1).

Movement 2:

Repeat the Movement 2 in Posture 9: Single Whip (Photo 11-2).

Insights: The same as Posture 9.

Posture 12: High Pat on Horse

Photo 12-1

Photo 12-2

Movement 1:

Step your right foot forward by half a step, bringing it closer to your left foot, then smoothly shift your weight onto your right leg. Simultaneously, open your right hand and bend your right arm at the elbow, moving your right hand above your right shoulder in a poised and ready position. As you make this transition, turn your left palm upward while keeping your left arm extended forward, maintaining a protective stance toward the east (Photo 12-1).

Movement 2:

Gently lift your left heel off the ground, placing only the toes on the floor to form a left empty stance. If necessary, adjust by moving the left foot slightly forward to maintain balance. Turn your torso slightly to the left while extending your right palm forward past your right ear in a controlled push toward the east, with the fingertips aligned at eye level and the elbow slightly lowered for stability. At the same time, move your left hand in a smooth downward curve toward the front of your left hip, with the palm facing upward, creating a harmonious and balanced motion. This movement integrates a blend of offense and defense (Photo 12-2).

Insights: *High Pat on Horse* is a powerful posture that particularly enhances energy flow through the six vertical foot meridians. The Liver (肝), Spleen, and Kidney (肾) meridians rise from the feet up the front torso, while the Bladder, Gallbladder (膽), and Stomach meridians descend from the head to the toes. The upright torso and forward-extended right arm, balanced with the empty left foot in front, create a dynamic stretch that facilitates energy release through the back Shu points to dispel stagnation. This posture also promotes spinal alignment and disc space, supporting lower back health and helping to prevent hunchbacks. In martial terms, the left hand draws or traps the opponent's arm, redirecting it to the side of your left hip, while the right hand delivers a fast, focused strike to the face—blending control with explosive intent.

Posture 13: Kick with Right Heel

Photo 13-1   Photo 13-2

Movement 1:

Ward off with your left hand in front of your chest, positioning the palm diagonally inward so that it crosses at the wrist with your right hand, whose palm faces outward. Maintain both arms rounded, creating a shield-like protective structure in front of you. Simultaneously, lift your left foot slightly off the ground, preparing for the next step. Hold this balanced stance momentarily, ensuring stability and control before transitioning (Photo 13-1).

Movement 2:

Gently separate your hands, moving them in a smooth downward curve with palms turning obliquely downward, as if redirecting an incoming force. At the same time, step your left foot forward toward the left front (northeast) and settle into a strong and rooted left bow stance. Keep your body aligned and centered, allowing your movement to flow naturally into the next transition (Photo 13-2).

Photo 13-3   Photo 13-4

Movement 3:

Continue the fluid motion of your hands in a downward-then-upward curve until your wrists cross once again in front of your chest, with your right hand on the outside and both palms facing inward. Maintain rounded arms, forming a shield-like ward-off protection. Simultaneously, lift your right knee up to abdomen height, balancing on your left leg in a stable left-leg roster stance, with your right foot toes pointing diagonally downward. Engage your core to maintain balance and stability in this poised position (Photo 13-3).

Movement 4:

Separate your hands, extending both arms sideways above shoulder with elbows slightly bent and palms turned outward. At the same time, execute a right front kick toward the southeast corner, keeping your gaze focused on your right foot. The kicking force should be delivered to the right heel, with the ankle dorsiflexed for proper energy control. Coordinate your arm movements with the kick, ensuring your right arm remains above and parallel to your right leg, enhancing balance and control in this dynamic movement (Photo 13-4).

Insights: *Kick with Right Heel* integrates wellness, body conditioning, and martial arts into a single dynamic posture. From a wellness perspective, the movement begins with the arms closing in front of the torso, as if gathering fresh qi through the Mu points. As the arms extend upward and outward—with palms turning out—it releases tension through the back Shu points and hand-Yin channels, while also stimulating the Triple Burner (三焦) system. This regulates energy flow across the upper (lungs and heart), middle (stomach and spleen), and lower (kidneys and reproductive organs) regions, promoting systemic harmony. From a fitness standpoint, the posture enhances whole-body elasticity and flexibility. The raised arms encourage spinal extension, while the kicking leg activates the Bladder meridian, stretching the posterior chain for leg elasticity. In martial application, the arms deflect or parry incoming force, creating an opening for the right heel to deliver a focused and powerful kick—merging softness with explosive intent in true Tai Chi fashion.

Posture 14: Strike Opponent's Ears with Both Fists

Photo 14-1   Photo 14-2

Movement 1:

Draw your left hand inward to meet your right hand in front of your chest, forming a protective ward-off posture. Simultaneously, pull back your right leg before placing your right foot down toward the southeast corner in a controlled landing. As you do so, lower both hands in a smooth, downward motion, as if deflecting an incoming force. Keep your focus toward your right front corner, ensuring stability and awareness of your stance (Photo 14-1).

Movement 2:

Shift your weight forward onto your right leg, transitioning into a strong right bow stance. At the same time, clench both palms into fists and rotate your arms inward before delivering an upward and forward strike, with fists reaching eye height and positioned approximately ten inches apart. Maintain proper structure by keeping the shoulders relaxed, elbows slightly lowered, and arms rounded to channel strength effectively while preserving the integrity of the movement (Photo 14-2).

Insights: *Strike Opponent's Ears with Both Fists* blends internal energy activation, structural conditioning, and martial application in a compact yet powerful movement. From a wellness perspective, this posture stimulates the Governing Vessel (督脉) along the spine, which governs the circulation of Yang energy throughout the body. The rounded "lobster claw" arm shape and expanded back help activate both the Governing Vessel and the paired back Shu points, encouraging energy flow and releasing deep-seated stagnation. This posture reflects the Tai Chi principle of "qi adhering to the spine" (氣貼脊背), essential for cultivating inner strength and resilience. From a fitness perspective, the diagonal stretch from feet to fists enhances the body's spring-like qualities—improving elasticity and structural integration. In martial application, the posture is to parry downward incoming force followed by a simultaneous double-fist strike aimed at the opponent's ears—a disorienting technique delivered with rooted strength and explosive expansion.

Posture 15: Kick with Left Heel

Photo 15-1   Photo 15-2

Movement 1:

Sink your right hip while relaxing your left hip, drawing your left heel inward and turn your right toes inward to adjust your stance. At the same time, open both fists, extending your right hand in a ward-off motion toward the southeast corner while turning your torso to the left. Simultaneously, guide your left palm in a smooth roll-back motion toward the northwest as you shift your weight onto your left foot. Maintain a rounded structure with both arms, keeping the elbows slightly sunk to sustain a balanced ward-off energy (Photo 15-1).

Movement 2:

Continue the movement by circling both hands in a downward-inward-upward arc until the wrists cross in front of your chest, palms facing inward with the left palm positioned on the outside. This creates a protective, shield-like structure with your forearms. At the same time, shift your weight onto your right leg and lift your left leg, keeping your toes pointing diagonally toward the floor. Maintain a steady posture and direct your gaze toward the northwest corner (Photo 15-2).

Movement 3:

Repeat the Movement 4 in Posture 13: Kick with Right Heel, and reversing "right" and "left" (Photo 15-3).

Photo 15-3

Insights: The same as Posture 13.

Posture 16: Golden Rooster Stands on One Leg - Left

Photo 16-1　　　　　　　　Photo 16-2

Movement 1:

Draw your left foot inward and turn your torso slightly to the right. You may let your left toes touch the floor briefly for balance or keep the foot lifted if your stability allows. Simultaneously, form a hook with your right hand while moving your left palm inward past your face, positioning it in front of your right chest to protect the right rib area (Photo 16-1).

Movement 2:

Lower your weight onto your right leg, bending into a deep crouch while extending your left leg sideways toward the west, slightly angled outward toward the southwest. At the same time, sweep your left palm in a downward curve along the inner side of your left leg. Keep your weight centered over your right heel while maintaining a subtle arch in your left knee for joint protection. Extend your right hook hand dynamically toward the northeast (Photo 16-2).

Photo 16-3　　　　　　　　Photo 16-4

Movement 3:

Turn your left toes slightly outward and pivot your right toes inward as you straighten your right leg and bend your left knee into a stable left bow stance to shift your weight onto your left foot. Simultaneously, raise your left hand to the west at chin height with the palm facing right. Meanwhile, your right hand lowers behind your right hip still in the form of a hook with fingertips bunched and pointing backward. Maintain a relaxed yet engaged posture, keeping your spine extended and shoulders down to support smooth energy flow (Photo 16-3).

Movement 4:

Turn your left toes slightly more outward to establish a firm base, then raise your right knee in front of your torso, maintaining balance and stability. At the same time, open your right hand into a palm and swing it above your right knee, keeping the elbow sunk and the fingertips aligned at nose height, with the palm facing left. Meanwhile, lower your left palm to the side of your left thigh, palm facing downward, in a controlled and grounded position. This iconic posture, known as the "Golden Rooster Stands on One Leg," embodies balance, focus, and strength (Photo 16-4).

Insights: *Left Lower Form and Stand on One Leg* beautifully embodies the Tai Chi principle of Yin-Yang harmonization—shifting from a low, grounded posture like a creeping snake to a tall, balanced stance like a rooster standing high. From a wellness perspective, the low form deeply stretches the leg and opens the three foot-Yin meridians, promoting energy circulation from the feet upward. Transitioning into the one-legged stance encourages energy to sink through the foot-Yang meridians, grounding the body, while also drawing earth energy upward through the inner legs to the front of the chest—supporting internal balance and organ vitality. It is especially good for the kidney meridian, gathering earth energy through the "bubbling well" point located at the bottom of the front part of the foot. From a fitness standpoint, this posture trains hip compressibility, leg elasticity, and overall balance, enhancing joint mobility, stability, and bone density. The dynamic height shift also builds core strength and coordination. In martial application, the low posture draws the opponent's energy downward, breaking their root or focus, while the rise into one leg allows for a sudden upward counterstrike—using the hand, elbow, knee, or foot with precision and explosive power.

Posture 17: Golden Rooster Stands on One Leg - Right

Photo 17-1

Photo 17-2

Movement 1:

Land down your right foot in front of the left foot with toes on the floor, and turn your body to the left while parrying your right palm in an inward and downward curve to the front of your left shoulder. At the same time, pivoting on the toes of your left foot to turn your left heel a bit inward, and ward off your left palm sideways toward the southeast and turn it into a hook hand above your shoulder. Look to the west (Photo 17-1).

Photo 17-3

Movement 2:

Repeat the Movement 2 in Posture 16: Left Lower Form and Stand on One Leg, and reversing "right" and "left" (Photo 17-2).

Movement 3:

Repeat the Movement 3 and 4 in Posture 16: Left Lower Form and Stand on One Leg, and reversing "right" and "left" (Photo 17-3, 17-4).

Insights: The same as Posture 16.

Photo 17-4

Posture 18: Fair Lady Works with Shuttles on Both Sides

Photo 18-1   Photo 18-2

Movement 1:

Step your left foot forward with your toes pointing outward toward the southwest corner. As you do so, lower your left palm in front of your left shoulder, palm facing downward. Simultaneously, shift your weight onto your left foot while moving your right hand toward your lower abdomen, palm facing upward, forming a "Hold Ball" posture (Photo 18-1).

Movement 2:

Rotate your body to the right and step your right foot forward toward the northwest corner. Raise your right hand to the front of your right temple, turning the palm obliquely upward and forward. At the same time, guide your left palm in a smooth, leftward and downward arc to the side of your left ribs. Without pausing, shift your weight onto your right leg, settling into a right bow stance and push your left palm forward and upward in front of your chest toward the northwest corner (Photo 18-2).

Photo 18-3　　　　　　　　　　Photo 18-4

Movement 3:

Turn your right foot slightly outward, adjusting your balance as you draw your left foot in beside your right, with only the toes touching the floor. Simultaneously, lower your right hand in front of your right shoulder, palm facing downward, while moving your left hand in a curved motion back toward your lower abdomen, palm facing upward. This movement brings you into a stable and centered "Hold a Ball" posture (Photo 18-3).

Movement 4:

Repeat the Movement 2 and reversing "right" and "left" (Photo 18-4).

Insights: *Fair Lady Works with Shuttles on Both Sides.* From a wellness perspective, the "holding the ball" gesture gathers fresh qi into the Mu points on the front torso, while the extended pushing hand activates the back Shu points, helping to release internal organ stagnation and promote energetic balance. This coordinated action supports the smooth circulation of qi throughout the body. Particularly, this posture benefits the liver meridians, because the palm is pushed out from the ribside where the energy point, Qimen, "Gate of Cycles" (期門穴) located. It can unblock stagnation to alleviate hypochondriac pain, chest tightness, anger, depression, and sighing from emotional blockages. In terms of fitness, the pushing motion—driven by legs and the waist's rotational force—enhances arm elasticity and develops integrated power through the torso and limbs. The spiraling movement also trains your body's twistability and coordinated expansion, improving mobility and structural cohesion. From a martial perspective, this posture maintains protection of the centerline while using one arm to parry and redirect incoming force upward, followed by a precise push-strike with the other arm—demonstrating Tai Chi's ability to blend softness and control with focused power.

Posture 19: Needle at Sea Bottom

Photo 19-1　　　　　　　　　Photo 19-2

Movement 1:

Step your right foot forward by half a step and shift your weight onto it. Then, move your left foot slightly forward, keeping only the toes touching the floor as you settle into a left empty stance. Simultaneously, turn your torso slightly to the right while guiding your right hand in a downward curve past your abdomen, then upward to the side of your right ear, palm facing obliquely forward. At the same time, move your left hand in a gentle arc downward to the front of your abdomen (Photo 19-1).

Movement 2:

Advance your left foot slightly forward, keeping only the toes touching the floor, and turn your torso to the left while bending your torso by hinging forward at the hips. As you do so, extend your right palm downward and forward in a controlled thrust, while positioning your left palm near the side of your left knee for coordination and balance (Photo 19-2).

Insights: *Needle at Sea Bottom* is a deep internal movement that integrates energy flow, structural conditioning, and martial function with focused intent. From a wellness perspective, the twisting and forward-bending motion directly stimulates the kidneys, located in the lower back, and activates the Bladder meridian that runs along the spine. In TCM, the Kidney-Bladder pair governs the body's fluid balance and foundational energy. This posture promotes smooth qi circulation through these channels, helping to prevent stagnation that can cause lower back pain and systemic imbalance—embodying the principle "where there is no flow, there is pain." (不通則痛). From a fitness perspective, the combined twist and downward reach stretches the spine, shoulders, and back arm chain, enhancing flexibility, spinal mobility, and core control. The rooted stance also strengthens the lower body and encourages hip compressibility. In martial application, the waist twist generates internal force, allowing the hands to execute techniques such as plucking, splitting, or joint locking and control—delivered from a grounded and spiraled structure with precision and power.

Posture 20: Fan Through the Back

Photo 20-1   Photo 20-2

Movement 1:

Straighten your torso while drawing your left foot back toward your right, keeping the toes just a few inches off the floor. At the same time, lift your right arm in a smooth upward motion, passing in front of your chest and rising to the front of your head. Simultaneously, move up your left palm and position it in front of your chest for a guarding pose (Photo 20-1).

Movement 2:

Without pausing, turn your torso slightly to the right as you step your left foot forward toward the west, shifting your weight onto it and settling into a stable left bow stance. As you transition, extend your left palm forward at shoulder height, fingers pointing upward, delivering a controlled push. Meanwhile, draw your right palm back to the outside of your right temple, with the palm facing obliquely upward and the thumb pointing downward (Photo 20-2).

Insights: *Fan Through the Back* harmonizes internal energy flow, body mechanics, and martial strategy with elegant precision. From a wellness perspective, this posture revitalizes the heart by opening the armpits, where the heart meridian originates and travels down the inner arm to the small finger. As the pinky side of both palms lead the expansion, qi flows smoothly through the chest and arms, helping to release stagnation and support cardiovascular health. In terms of fitness, the posture creates a powerful diagonal stretch between the right leg and left arm, enhancing spinal and shoulder elasticity. At the same time, the left leg and right arm form a stabilizing structure, with left hip compressibility serving as a rooted base that supports balance, strength, and dynamic alignment. From a martial arts perspective, the right hand initiates a parry and roll-back, neutralizing incoming force, while the left palm delivers a precise counter-strike. As the left foot steps in, it secures advantageous positioning—allowing you to control the center, dominate the space, and maintain structural superiority over the opponent.

Posture 21: Turn to Deflect, Parry and Punch

Photo 21-1   Photo 21-2

Movement 1:

Turn your body to the right, shifting your weight onto your right leg as you pivot your left foot inward. Then, transfer your weight back onto your left foot and draw your right foot close to your left, keeping only the toes touching the floor in a right empty stance. Simultaneously, sweep both arms in a rightward curve—clenching your right hand into a loose fist and lowering it toward your abdomen, while your left hand arcs across your head, positioning in front of your face in a guarded posture with both arms rounded (Photo 21-1).

Movement 2:

Slightly rotate your torso further to the right and deflect your right fist forward and diagonally to the southeast. At the same time, guide your left palm downward in a curved path past the front of your body, positioning it near your left hip. As you transition, withdraw your right foot briefly before stepping it out to the east, ensuring the toes point outward (Photo 21-2).

Photo 21-3   Photo 21-4

Movement 3:

Turn your body to the right and step your left foot forward toward the east. At the same time, execute a parrying motion with your left hand, sweeping it in a controlled, curved path from the left side upward to the front of your chest, with the palm angled slightly downward. Meanwhile, withdraw your right fist in a downward arc, bringing it close to the side of your right ribs in a poised and balanced stance (Photo 21-3).

Movement 4:

Step your left foot slightly forward, shifting your weight onto it as you settle into a stable left bow stance. Simultaneously, deliver a controlled punch with your right fist, extending it forward toward the east at upper chest height, with the thumb side facing upward. Keep your right arm slightly bent at the elbow to maintain structure and control. At the same time, withdraw your left palm to the side of your right elbow (Photo 21-4).

Insights: *Turn to Deflect, Parry and Punch* integrates emotional regulation, spring-like body mechanics, and decisive martial strategy into one powerful sequence. From a wellness perspective, the punch helps soothe liver qi stagnation, which in TCM is closely linked to anger regulation and detoxification. The movement starts from the foot, channels through the leg, and is driven by the waist, releasing from the ribside at the liver meridian's endpoint, Qi-men (期門)—the "Gate of Cycle." This provides a healthy outlet for frustration or rage, restoring emotional balance. Since chronic anger and liver dysfunction are mutually reinforcing, this posture helps break that cycle. From a fitness viewpoint, the posture mimics a coiling spring—the deflect and parry initiate a deep torso twist to the right, followed by a recoil and powerful twist to the left with the punch. This trains waist flexibility, coordinated leg drive, and the elastic recoil of the spine, arms, and legs, cultivating whole-body integration and dynamic power. In martial application, it exemplifies Tai Chi's strategy of redirecting with softness and countering with strength: parry the incoming force, step in with the left foot to gain positional advantage, and issue a decisive right fist strike from a rooted, aligned stance—blending structure, timing, and precision to neutralize the threat.

Posture 22: Apparent Closure

Photo 22-1　　　　　　　　　　Photo 22-2

Movement 1:

Move your left hand forward from beneath your right forearm while simultaneously opening your right fist. Shift your weight back onto your right leg, raising the toes of your left foot slightly off the floor. At the same time, separate your hands to shoulder width and draw them back toward your chest, palms facing upward and inward (Photo 22-1).

Movement 2:

Rotate your palms downward and press them in front of your abdomen before pushing them forward and upward toward the east until reaching shoulder height with palms facing forward. As you do this, shift your weight forward and bend your left knee, settling into a stable left bow stance. Keep your shoulders relaxed and allow your elbows to sink and ward off slightly outward, maintaining a balanced and powerful posture (Photo 22-2).

Insights: *Apparent Closure* blends energy regulation, structural conditioning, and martial strategy into a unified movement. From a wellness perspective, the posture begins by drawing the arms and torso inward with a deep inhale, as if gathering qi from nature into the Mu points at the front of the torso. As you exhale and push the palms and torso forward, it facilitates the release of internal stagnation through the Shu points along the back—supporting the organs and promoting smooth energy flow. From a fitness viewpoint, the extended right leg and outstretched arms train full-body elasticity, while the rooted left foot and compressed left hip create a strong, coiled foundation for leg strength and structural stability. In martial application, this posture is used to draw the opponent in, disrupting their balance and positioning them for a decisive double-palm strike—executed from a rooted, aligned body to project maximum force and control.

Posture 23: Cross Hands

Photo 23-1   Photo 23-2

Movement 1:

Sink your hips and bend your right leg, shifting your weight onto your right foot. As you turn your body to the right, pivot the toes of your left foot forward while slightly angling the toes of your right foot outward for improved balance. Following the body's natural turn, extend both arms outward in an upper horizontal curve just above shoulder level, keeping the elbows slightly bent and palms facing forward in a poised, open posture (Photo 23-1).

Movement 2:

Lower your hands in a curved motion from the outside and cross them at the wrists in front of your belly. Then, shift your weight onto your left leg and bring your right foot toward your left until both feet are relatively parallel and shoulder-width apart. At the same time, lift palms in front of your chest with rounded arms, allowing the elbows to sink slightly and ward off gently. Position your left hand closer to your body, with both palms facing inward, maintaining a centered and balanced stance (Photo 23-2).

Insights: *Cross Hands* symbolizes the closing and sealing of energy, integrating wellness, structural conditioning, and self-defense. From a wellness perspective, the posture begins with an open-armed stretch that opens the Mu points on the front torso—gathering fresh qi from nature. The subsequent cross-handed closure helps seal and preserve that energy within the body, supporting internal harmony and calm. From a fitness standpoint, the expansive arm opening resembles a bird spreading its wings, enhancing shoulder and chest elasticity. The closing embrace offers a horizontal stretch across the back. In martial applications, the arms first ward off an incoming force, then cross in front of the chest to form a shield-like defense—protecting the centerline while maintaining structural readiness for transition into the next move.

Posture 24: Closing Form

Photo 24-1

Photo 24-2

Movement 1:

Extend your palms forward and separate them to shoulder width with elbows sink slightly (Photo 24-1).

Movement 2:

Lower palms to the side of your hips, and bring your left foot close to your right foot to finish the form (Photo 24-2)

Insights: *Closing Form* (收式) is the final seal of a Tai Chi session, guiding the transition from movement to stillness. From a wellness perspective, it channels the cultivated qi inward, allowing it to settle into the lower dantian for nourishment and integration—preventing energy dissipation and supporting internal balance. Physically, the posture promotes calm alignment and rootedness, signaling the body to shift from dynamic activity to stillness and grounding, while maintaining relaxed structural integrity. Martially, it represents the return to neutral readiness—a non-combative state where force is withheld, yet the body remains centered and prepared. It completes the Tai Chi cycle: from opening to connect with nature's energy, to closing and sealing it within.

玉女穿梭

Fair Lady Works with Shuttle

Part II

Tai Chi Double-Clubbell in Form 24

Posture 1: Opening Form

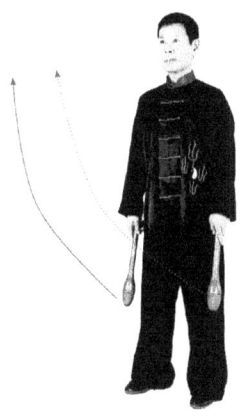

Photo 1-1

Photo 1-2

Movement 1:

Stand facing the south and step your left foot sideways so that your feet are shoulder-width apart, ensuring your toes point relatively forward. Allow your hands to hang naturally by your sides with the clubbell head pointing down. Keep your gaze directed forward (Photo 1-1).

Note: The lines and arrows in figure 1 indicate the movement paths for the next photo, which is explained in Movement 2. This pattern continues for all subsequent illustrations.

Movement 2:

Raise your arms forward and upward until clubbells reach shoulder height, keeping arms naturally extended and relaxed, avoid locking your elbows to maintain a sense of fluidity and readiness (Photo 1-2).

Photo 1-3

Movement 3:

Sink your hips and bend your knees slightly, grounding yourself in a stable stance. Lower your elbows and gently strike the clubbells downward to about hip height. Let the weight of the clubbell to elastic your arm, and let your posture convey calmness and stability (Photo 1-3).

Posture 2: Part Wild Horse's Mane

Photo 2-1   Photo 2-2

Movement 1:

Rotate your right-hand clubbell in a curved motion from your right side while simultaneously guiding the left-hand clubbell downward in a small arc. The clubbells trace a counterclockwise circular pattern, cultivating a sense of harmony and balance. Continue the movement until the right-hand clubbell naturally rests in front of your chest and the left-hand clubbell aligns near your lower belly. Slightly shift your left foot inward, allowing only the toes to lightly touch the floor for added stability and readiness. At the conclusion of the motion, both clubbells are in a guarding position to protect your centerline, ensuring your body stays grounded and centered (Photo 2-1).

Movement 2:

Turn your body to the left and step your left foot outward to the east. Shift your weight onto your left foot and bend your left knee to form a bow stance. Simultaneously, strike out your left-hand clubbell to face height and lower your right-hand clubbell to the side of your right hip. Keep your gaze focused on your left-hand clubbell (Photo 2-2).

Photo 2-3

Photo 2-4

Movement 3:

Shift your weight back, lift your left toes, and turn them outward before placing your entire foot on the floor. Then, rotate your body to the left and step your right foot beside your left. Simultaneously, rotate your left wrist inward in a clockwise circle to lower the left-hand clubbell in front of your chest. At the same time, circle your right-hand clubbell in a clockwise coil spring drilling motion toward the front of your belly. The clubbells maintain a protection of your centerline (Photo 2-3).

Photo 2-5

Movement 4:

Turn your body to the right slightly and step your right foot forward to the east and shift your weight onto your right foot and bend your right knee to form a bow stance. Simultaneously, strike out your right-hand clubbell to face height and parry your left-hand clubbell to the front of your belly. Keep your gaze focused on your right-hand clubbell (Photo 2-4).

Photo 2-6

Movement 5:

Repeat Movement 3 and 4 reversing "left" and "right" (Photo 2-5 and Photo 2-6).

Posture 3: White Crane Spreading Its Wings

Photo 3-1   Photo 3-2

Movement 1:

Step your right foot half a step closer to your left foot while slightly turning your torso to the left. Parry the left-hand clubbell to the front of your right shoulder, and parry the right-hand clubbell to the front of your left hip to form a crossing diagonal pose protecting your front centerline (Photo 3-1).

Movement 2:

Move your left foot slightly forward, placing only the toes on the floor to form a left empty stance. Simultaneously, strike your right-hand clubbell above the front of your forehead and parry your left-hand clubbell to the front of your left hip in curved paths, keeping both arms slightly rounded. You are relatively facing the east (Photo 3-2).

Posture 4: Brush Knee on Both Sides

Photo 4-1   Photo 4-2

Movement 1:

Parry your right-hand clubbell in a downward arc, guided by the twisting of your torso, from the front of your forehead to the side of your right hip. Simultaneously, move your left-hand clubbell in an inward and upward arc from the side of your left hip to the front of your face to form a closed defensive pose (Photo 4-1).

Movement 2:

Step forward with your left foot to the east into a left bow stance. Simultaneously, circle your right-hand clubbell backward and upward from the rear right corner, above your right shoulder, and strike it forward to the east at face height. Sink your right shoulder and keep your right elbow slightly down. At the same time, parry your left-hand clubbell in an arc through your centerline to the side of your left knee. This movement creates a "brush away and strike out" pose (Photo 4-2).

Photo 4-3   Photo 4-4

Movement 3:

Shift your weight slightly to raise the toes of your left foot, turning your torso a bit to the left. Then, move up your right foot to the side of your left foot with the ball touching the floor. At the same time, move your right-hand clubbell inward and backward toward your chest to protect your centerline, while moving your left-hand clubbell in a parrying motion to the front side of your left hip (Photo 4-3).

Movement 4:

Parry your right-hand clubbell downward in a curved path along your centerline to the front of your right knee. Simultaneously, step your right foot forward to the east into a right bow stance. At the same time, circle your left-hand clubbell backward and upward in an arc from the side of your left hip to the side of your left ear, then strike it forward to the east at nose height. Sink your left shoulder and keep your left elbow slightly down (Photo 4-4).

Photo 4-5   Photo 4-6

Movement 5:

Repeat Movement 3 and 4 reversing "left" and "right" (Photo 4-5 and 4-6).

Posture 5: Playing a Guitar

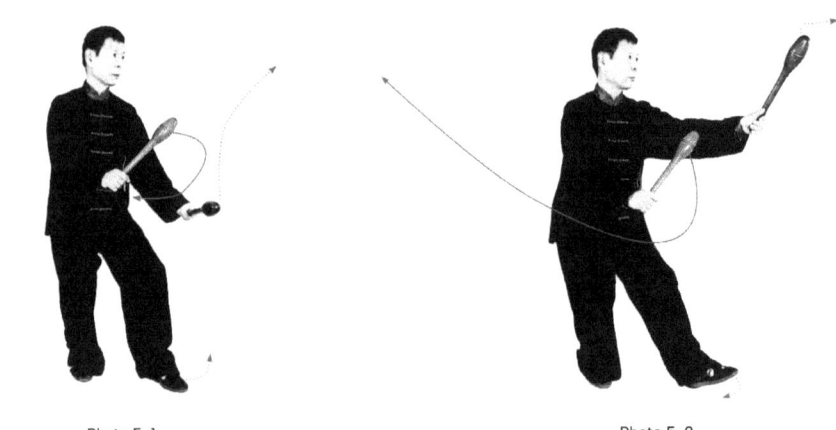

Photo 5-1   Photo 5-2

Movement 1:

Step your right foot half a step closer to your left heel. Simultaneously, withdraw your right-hand clubbell toward the center of your chest in a downward and inward path, while moving your left-hand clubbell a bit forward and inward in front of your belly. This posture is regarded as a closing and protective pose (Photo 5-1).

Movement 2:

Step your left foot forward a bit to the east, placing the heel on the floor and toes up with the knee slightly bent to form a left empty stance. At the same time, extend your left-hand clubbell forward and upward to face height and bring your right-hand clubbell toward the left elbow. Sink both hips, lengthen the spine, and lift the head, keeping the shoulders and elbows relaxed and down (Photo 5-2).

Posture 6: Repulse Monkey

Photo 6-1   Photo 6-2

Movement 1:

Turn your torso slightly to the right and turn your toes of your left foot slightly inward, parry your right-hand clubbell in a downward curve past your abdomen and then backward and upward to shoulder height. Simultaneously, extend your left-hand clubbell forward slightly, parrying it gently to the left. At the end of the motion, both arms should be wide open, with elbows slightly bent. First, glance at your right hand while it is going back, then shift your gaze to your left-hand clubbell in front of you (Photo 6-1).

Movement 2:

Step your left foot back and turn the heel of your right foot outward. Simultaneously, bend your right arm and draw your right-hand clubbell past your right ear before striking it forward in front of your chest, while your left-hand clubbell parries in a downward curve toward your left abdomen (Photo 6-2).

Photo 6-3   Photo 6-4

Movement 3:

Move your left-hand clubbell in a downward and backward curve past the outside of your left hip before raising it to shoulder height. Extend your right palm forward to the east and slightly parry outward, forming an open-arms posture with both elbows slightly bent. First, glance at your left-hand clubbell as it moves back, then shift your gaze to your right-hand clubbell in front of you (Photo 6-3).

Movement 4:

Step your right foot back and twist the heel of your left foot outward to prevent the strain of your left knee. Simultaneously, bend your left arm and draw your left-hand clubbell past your left ear before striking it forward in front of your chest, while your right-hand clubbell parries in a downward curve toward your right abdomen (Photo 6-4).

Photo 6-5   Photo 6-6

Movement 5:
Repeat Movement 1 and 2 (Photo 6-5 and 6-6).

Photo 6-7 Photo 6-8

Movement 6:
Repeat Movement 3 and 4 (Photo 6-7 and 6-8).

Photo 6-9

Movement 7:
Repeat Movement 1 (Photo 6-9).

Posture 7: Grasp the Bird's Tail - Left

Photo 7-1   Photo 7-2

Movement 1:

Withdraw your left foot toward your right foot, with the ball of your left foot lightly touching the floor to form a left empty stance. Simultaneously, move your right-hand clubbell passing by your right ear to the front of your chest, while your left-hand clubbell parries in a downward curve in front of your belly. Clubbells form a closing defensive pose guarding your centerline (Photo 7-1).

Movement 2:

Step your left foot forward to the east, bending the knee into a left bow stance. Simultaneously, parry your right-hand clubbell in a downward curve to the side of your right hip, while moving your left-hand clubbell in front of your chest, as if warding off an incoming force. Keep both arms rounded, ensuring the movement and separation of the clubbells are coordinated (Photo 7-2).

Photo 7-3   Photo 7-4

Movement 3:

Turn your torso slightly to the left as you extend your left-hand clubbell forward a bit to the east, and bring your right-hand clubbell upward to the front of your chest to take the guarding center position. Although it appears as a brief pause, continue fluidly by turning your torso to the right while parrying both hand's clubbell, in a curved motion outward and downward, then upward to the front of your right shoulder. As you do this, shift your weight onto your right foot (Photo 7-3).

Movement 4:

Turn your torso left and align yourself to face east, while turning your left-hand clubbell horizontal and moving it in front of your chest. At the same time, close in your right-hand clubbell and place it on the top of the left-hand clubbell to form a cross shape protection. As you do this, shift your weight forward onto your left leg, transitioning into a left bow stance. Maintain a rounded shape with both arms and press both hands forward toward the east in a controlled and harmonious motion. Keep your gaze directed toward the east, embodying focus and intent of pressing (Photo 7-4).

Photo 7-5

Movement 5:

Extend the clubbells forward slightly and separate them to shoulder width apart. Gradually shift your weight back onto your right leg, drawing both hand's clubbells back and in a smooth downward curve to the front of your abdomen to form a protective and grounded pose. You may lift the toes of your left foot slightly off the floor, facilitating the weight shift to your back leg. Maintain a relaxed but focused posture (Photo 7-5).

Photo 7-6

Movement 6:

Transfer your weight onto your left leg, transitioning into a stable left bow stance. Simultaneously, strike both clubbells forward in a smooth upward curve until they reach shoulder height. Maintain a steady and flowing motion, keeping your arms slightly bent at elbows and relaxed. Direct your gaze straight ahead to the east, projecting focus and intent while maintaining balance and stability in your stance (Photo 7-6).

Posture 8: Grasp the Bird's Tail - Right

Photo 8-1

Photo 8-2

Movement 1:

Shift your weight onto your right leg as you gently turn your torso to the right. At the same time, sweep your right-hand clubbell in a smooth horizontal arc, slightly upward, toward the west as if deflecting an incoming force. Simultaneously, turn the toes of your left foot a bit inward, and the heel of your right foot inward to protect your knees from strain. Turn your left-hand clubbell head pointing to the south with the arm still extended, maintaining warding-off toward the east, Focus on coordinating your torso and arm movements fluidly while grounding your stance (Photo 8-1).

Movement 2:

Turn the toes of your left foot inward, and shift your weight onto your left foot, and bring your right foot beside your left, with the ball of your right foot lightly touching the floor to form a right empty stance. Simultaneously, parry your right-hand clubbell in a downward curve toward your abdomen, while your left-hand clubbell moves inward to the front of your chest. Together, the clubbells form a protection of your centerline. This posture symbolizes a closing defensive stance, embodying readiness and control, while maintaining balance and focus (Photo 8-2).

Photo 8-3

Photo 8-4

Photo 8-5

Photo 8-6

Photo 8-7

Movement 3:

Repeat the Movement 2, 3, 4, 5, and 6 in Posture 7: Grasp the Bird's Tail - Left, and reversing "left" and "right" (Photo 8-3, 8-4, 8-5, 8-6, and 8-7).

Posture 9: Single Whip

Photo 9-1   Photo 9-2

Movement 1:

Sink your right hip and shift weight toward your left foot while turning your right toes inward. At the same time, rotate your torso to the left, smoothly carrying the clubbells leftward—your left-hand clubbell tracing an upward arc past your face to guard to your right front, while your right-hand clubbell follows a downward curve across the front of your crotch. Then, turn your left heel inward to protect your left knee from strain (Photo 9-1).

Movement 2:

Shift your weight onto your right foot as you draw your left foot beside your right. As your weight transitions, allow your arms to continue their circular motion from your left to the right, parring your left-hand clubbell downward to rest in front of your right ribs. Simultaneously, your right-hand clubbell arcs upward past your face toward the right front corner. Maintain a sense of balance and energy flow throughout the movement, ensuring each transition is seamless and connected (Photo 9-2).

Photo 9-3

Movement 3:

Turn your torso to the left, step your left foot forward to the east into a strong and balanced left bow stance. Simultaneously, strike your left-hand clubbell in a whipping motion from your right rib side across your face to the left at shoulder height. Following this leftward motion, execute your right-hand clubbell a controlled parry toward the southwest corner to make a protective barrier, and maintain a counterbalance and structural integrity within the form (Photo 9-3).

Posture 10: Wave Hands Like Clouds

Photo 10-1

Photo 10-2

Movement 1:

Sink your right hip and gently shift your weight gradually onto your right foot while simultaneously turning your torso to the right and warding off your right-hand clubbell toward your right front. As your body rotates, parry your left-hand clubbell in a downward curve toward the front of your right hip, maintaining a relaxed yet intentional posture. At the same time, turn your left foot inward a bit to ensure a stable stance. (Photo 10-1).

Movement 2:

Parry your right-hand clubbell in a downward curve toward the front of your left hip as your turn torso to the left. Simultaneously, parry your left-hand clubbell in an upward arc, across your face gradually rotating your left wrist outward until the clubbell to your left front to form a protection. As you turn your torso to the left, shift your weight onto your left foot and bring your right foot in, placing it beside your left foot for a moment of centered stability (Photo 10-2).

Photo 10-3   Photo 10-4

Movement 3:

Sweep your right-hand clubbell in a smooth, upward curve toward the front of your left shoulder, maintaining the arm rounded and continue the circle with your torso turning to right to parry the clubbell past your face to the right side while gradually rotating your right wrist outward. As this unfolds, shift your weight onto your right foot and parry your left-hand clubbell in a downward arc toward the front of your right hip, keeping your arm relaxed yet engaged. As your weight shifts, step your left foot out to the east with intention, creating a stable foundation for the next movement (Photo 10-3).

Movement 4:

Repeat Movement 2 (Photo 10-4).

Photo 10-5   Photo 10-6

Movement 5:

Repeat Movement 3 and 4 (Photo 10-5, 10-6).

Posture 11: Single Whip

Photo 11-1   Photo 11-2

Movement 1:

Sweeping your right-hand clubbell in an upward curve from the front of your left hip, across your face, to the front of your right shoulder creating a protective and expansive motion. Simultaneously, lower your left-hand clubbell to guard near the front of your left hip, maintaining a balanced and defensive posture. Shift your weight onto your right foot while turning your torso slightly to the right. At the same time, parry your left palm inward to align with the front of your right ribs, ensuring a compact and protective stance. Lift your left heel lightly off the ground, keeping your toes touching the floor, positioning yourself in a poised, ready-to-step-out left empty stance (Photo 11-1).

Movement 2:

Repeat the Movement 3 in Posture 9: Single Whip (Photo 11-2).

Posture 12: High Pat on Horse

Photo 12-1   Photo 12-2

Movement 1:

Step your right foot forward by half a step, bringing it closer to your left foot, then smoothly shift your weight onto your right leg and lift up your left heel to form a left empty stance. Simultaneously, parry your right-hand clubbell forward to the front of your chest. As you make this transition, rotate your left wrist inward to bring the left-hand clubbell half way back and down to maintain a protective pose toward the east (Photo 12-1).

Movement 2:

Turn your torso slightly to the left while striking your right-hand clubbell forward and a bit upward toward the east. At the same time, parry your left-hand clubbell in a smooth downward curve toward the front of your left hip, creating a harmonious and balanced motion with your right hand. This movement integrates a blend of offense and defense (Photo 12-2).

Posture 13: Kick with Right Heel

Photo 13-1   Photo 13-2

Movement 1:

Bend your right wrist to turn the right-hand clubbell head pointing diagonally to the northeast corner, and at the same time, move up your left-hand clubbell in front of your chest, positioning it on top of the right-hand clubbell, diagonally pointing to the southeast corner. The clubbells cross with each other. Maintain both arms rounded, creating a shield-like protective structure in front of you. Simultaneously, lift your left knee to prepare for the next step. Hold this balanced stance momentarily, ensuring stability and control before transitioning (Photo 13-1).

Movement 2:

Separate your hands, moving the clubbells in a smooth curve opening out with both wrists rotating outward, as if to redirect an incoming force and maintain the warding off energy by keeping both arms rounded. At the same time, step your left foot forward toward the northeast and settle into a strong and rooted left bow stance (Photo 13-2).

Photo 13-3　　　　　　　　　　Photo 13-4

Movement 3:

Continue the fluid motion of your hands to move the clubbells in a downward-then-upward curve until they cross once again in front of your chest, with your right-hand clubbell on the outside. Maintain rounded arms, forming a shield-like ward-off protection. Simultaneously, lift your right knee up to abdomen height, balancing on your left leg in a stable left-leg rooster stance, with your right foot toes pointing diagonally downward. Engage your core to maintain balance and stability in this poised position (Photo 13-3).

Movement 4:

Separate your hands, strike both clubbells sideways at shoulder height with elbows slightly bent. At the same time, execute a right front kick toward the southeast corner, keeping your gaze focused on your right foot. The kicking force should be delivered to the right heel. Coordinate your arm movements with the kick, ensuring your right arm remains above and parallel to your right leg. Maintain balance and control in this dynamic movement (Photo 13-4).

Posture 14: Strike Opponent's Ears with Both Fists

Photo 14-1   Photo 14-2

Movement 1:

Draw your left-hand clubbell inward to meet your right-hand clubbell in front of your face, forming a protective ward-off posture. Simultaneously, pull back your right leg before placing your right foot down toward the southeast corner in a controlled landing. As you do so, parry both clubbells in a smooth, downward motion, as if deflecting an incoming force. Keep your focus toward your right front corner, ensuring stability and awareness of your stance (Photo 14-1).

Movement 2:

Shift your weight forward onto your right leg, transitioning into a strong right bow stance. Simultaneously, strike upward and forward with both clubbells, reaching eye height and positioning them approximately ten inches apart. Maintain proper structure by keeping your shoulders relaxed, elbows slightly lowered, and arms rounded to channel strength effectively while preserving the integrity of the movement (Photo 14-2).

Part II: Tai Chi Double-Clubbell in Form 24

Posture 15: Kick with Left Heel

Photo 15-1

Photo 15-2

Movement 1:

Sink your right hip while relaxing your left hip, drawing your left heel inward and turn your right toes inward to adjust your stance. At the same time, parry your right-hand clubbell toward the southeast corner while turning your torso to the left. Simultaneously, parry your left-hand clubbell toward the northwest as you shift your weight onto your left foot. Maintain a rounded structure with both arms and keeping the elbows slightly sunk to sustain a balanced ward-off energy (Photo 15-1).

Movement 2:

Circle both of your hands in a downward-inward-upward arc until the clubbells cross in front of your chest, with the left-hand clubbell positioned on the outside. This creates a protective, shield-like structure with the clubbells. At the same time, shift your weight onto your right leg and lift the left knee toward your belly, keeping your toes pointing diagonally toward the floor. Maintain a steady rooster standing on one foot posture and direct your gaze toward the northwest corner (Photo 15-2).

Photo 15-3

Movement 1:

Repeat the Movement 4 in Posture 13: Kick with Right Heel, and reversing "right" and "left" (Photo 15-3).

Posture 16: Golden Rooster Stands on One Leg - Left

Photo 16-1   Photo 16-2

Movement 1:

Draw your left foot inward close to your right leg, and you may let your left toes touch the floor briefly for balance or keep the foot lifted if your stability allows. Simultaneously, bend your right wrist to block the right-hand clubbell in front of your right shoulder while parrying your left-hand clubbell inward past your face, positioning it in front of your right chest to protect the right rib area (Photo 16-1).

Movement 2:

Lower your weight onto your right foot, bending your right knee into a deep crouch while extending your left leg sideways toward the west, angled slightly outward toward the southwest. Simultaneously, strike with your left-hand clubbell in a downward curve along the inner side of your left leg. Keep your weight centered over your right heel while maintaining a subtle arch in your left knee for joint protection. At the same time, parry your right-hand clubbell toward the northeast with the head pointing diagonally downward (Photo 16-2).

Photo 16-3 Photo 16-4

Movement 3:

Rise from the low form by shifting your weight onto your left foot and straightening your right leg. Pivot your right toes inward as you bend your left knee into a stable left bow stance. Simultaneously, flex your left wrist to pop the left-hand clubbell head upward, warding off to the west at chin height. Meanwhile, parry your right-hand clubbell behind your right hip, bending your right wrist to keep the clubbell head diagonally up on your lower back. Maintain a relaxed yet engaged protective posture (Photo 16-3).

Movement 4:

Turn your left toes slightly more outward to establish a firm base, then raise your right knee in front of your torso, maintaining balance and stability. At the same time, parry your left-hand clubbell down to the front of your left thigh in a controlled and protective position. Meanwhile, turn out your right-hand clubbell from your back and strike it upward and forward to the front of your chest. This iconic posture, known as the "Golden Rooster Stands on One Leg," embodies balance, focus, and strength (Photo 16-4).

Posture 17: Golden Rooster Stands on One Leg - Right

Photo 17-1

Photo 17-2

Movement 1:

Drop down your right foot, placing the ball of your foot on the floor in front of your left foot. Simultaneously, turn your body to the left and move your left foot heel inward to prevent the strain on your left knee while parrying your right-hand clubbell in an inward and downward curve toward the front of your left shoulder. At the same time, ward off with your left-hand clubbell, raising it upward and sideways toward the southeast above your left shoulder, with the clubbell head pointing diagonally downward. Keep your gaze directed toward the west (Photo 17-1).

Photo 17-3

Movement 2:

Repeat the Movement 2 in Posture 16: Left Lower Form and Stand on One Leg, and reversing "right" and "left" (Photo 17-2).

Movement 3:

Repeat the Movement 3 and 4 in Posture 16: Left Lower Form and Stand on One Leg, and reversing "right" and "left" (Photo 17-3, 17-4).

Photo 17-4

Posture 18: Fair Lady Works with Shuttles on Both Sides

Photo 18-1   Photo 18-2

Movement 1:

Step your left foot forward with your toes pointing outward toward the southwest corner. As you do so, parry your left-hand clubbell in an outward circle and return it in front of your left chest. Simultaneously, shift your weight onto your left foot while parrying your right-hand clubbell in an inward circle toward your lower abdomen. Clubbells form a protective position in front of your centerline (Photo 18-1).

Movement 2:

Rotate your body to the right and step your right foot forward toward the northwest corner. Simultaneously, parry your right-hand clubbell upward to the front of your right temple, turning your wrist outward and upward to form a strong protection. At the same time, guide your left-hand clubbell in a smooth, leftward, and downward arc to the side of your left ribs. Without pausing, shift your weight onto your right leg, settling into a right bow stance, and strike your left-hand clubbell forward and upward in front of your chest toward the northwest corner (Photo 18-2).

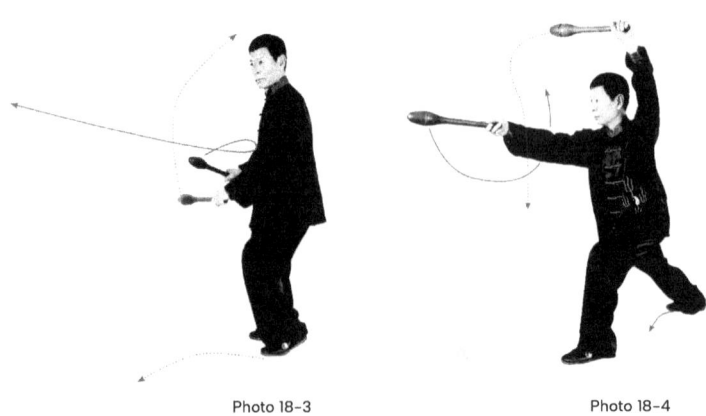

Photo 18-3　　　　　　　　　　Photo 18-4

Movement 3:

Turn your right foot slightly outward, adjusting your balance as you draw your left foot in beside your right, with only the toes touching the floor. Simultaneously, parry your right-hand clubbell inward and downward to the front of your chest, while parrying your left-hand clubbell in a curved motion back toward your lower abdomen. This movement brings you into a stable guarding your center position (Photo 18-3).

Movement 4:

Repeat the Movement 2 and reversing "right" and "left" (Photo 18-4).

Posture 19: Needle at Sea Bottom

Photo 19-1   Photo 19-2

Movement 1:

Step your right foot forward by half a step and shift your weight onto it. Then, move your left foot slightly forward, keeping only the ball touching the floor as you settle into a left empty stance. Simultaneously, turn your torso slightly to the right while sweeping your right-hand clubbell in a downward curve past your abdomen, then upward to the side of your right ear for protection. At the same time, parry your left-hand clubbell in a gentle arc downward to the front of your belly (Photo 19-1).

Movement 2:

Advance your left foot slightly forward, keeping only the toes touching the floor, and hinge forward at the hips. As you do so, strike your right-hand clubbell downward and forward, while parrying outward your left-hand clubbell near the side of your left knee for protection and balance (Photo 19-2).

Posture 20: Fan Through the Back

Photo 20-1   Photo 20-2

Movement 1:

Straighten your torso while drawing your left foot back toward your right, keeping your toes lightly touching the floor. At the same time, parry with your right-hand clubbell, positioning it diagonally in front of your chest for guard. Simultaneously, lift your left-hand clubbell and position it just a few inches behind the right-hand clubbell in a ready-to-act stance (Photo 20-1).

Movement 2:

Without pausing, turn your torso slightly to the right as you step your left foot forward toward the west, shifting your weight onto it and settling into a stable left bow stance. As you transition, parry your right-hand clubbell upward and backward to the outside of your right temple, with the clubbell head pointing to the south horizontally above your head. Meanwhile, deliver your left-hand clubbell a strike forward to the west at shoulder height (Photo 20-2).

Posture 21: Turn to Deflect, Parry and Punch

Photo 21-1   Photo 21-2

Movement 1:

Turn your body to the right, shifting your weight onto your right leg as you pivot your left toes inward. Then, transfer your weight back onto your left foot and draw your right foot close to your left, keeping only the ball of your foot touching the floor in a right empty stance. Simultaneously, sweep both clubbells in a rightward curve—your right-hand clubbell circles downward in front of your abdomen, while your left-hand clubbell arcs across your head, positioning in front of your chest with both arms rounded and hold the clubbells relatively in a horizontal guarded posture (Photo 21-1).

Movement 2:

Slightly rotate your torso further to the right and deflect your right-hand clubbell forward and diagonally to the southeast. At the same time, parry your left-hand clubbell downward in a curved path past the front of your chest, positioning it in front of your left hip. As you transition, step your right foot out to the east, ensuring the toes point outward diagonally to the southeast (Photo 21-2).

Photo 21-3   Photo 21-4

Movement 3:

Turn your body to the right and step your left foot forward toward the east, and keep your weight mainly on your right leg. At the same time, parry your left-hand clubbell in a controlled sweeping, curved path from the left side upward to the front of your chest, with the clubbell head pointing diagonally to the south. Meanwhile, withdraw your right-hand clubbell in a downward arc, bringing it close to the side of your right ribs in a poised and balanced stance (Photo 21-3).

Movement 4:

Shift your weight onto the left foot and twist your right heel back a bit to settle into a stable left bow stance. Simultaneously, parry down your left-hand clubbell slightly and strike your right-hand clubbell forward toward the east at upper chest height. Keep your right arm slightly bent at the elbow to maintain structure and control, and the left-hand clubbell just underneath your right forearm (Photo 21-4).

Posture 22: Apparent Closure

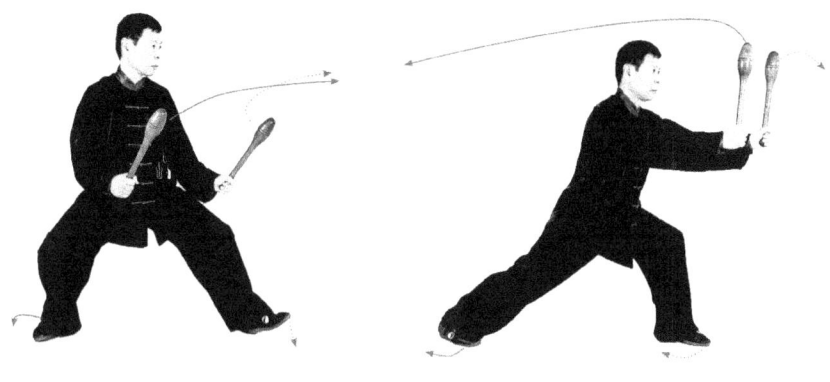

Photo 22-1   Photo 22-2

Movement 1:

Move your left-hand clubbell forward from beneath your right forearm while simultaneously parrying your right-hand clubbell outward and keep the clubbells about shoulder width apart. Shift your weight back onto your right leg, raising the toes of your left foot slightly off the floor. At the same time, draw the clubbells back toward your chest in an upward-then-downward curve (Photo 22-1).

Movement 2:

Push the clubbells forward and upward toward the east, with the clubbell heads pointing upward. As you do this, shift your weight forward, pressing down your left toes and bending your left knee while twisting your right heel backward to settle into a stable left bow stance. Keep your shoulders relaxed, allowing your elbows to sink and ward off slightly outward, maintaining a balanced and powerful posture (Photo 22-2).

Posture 23: Cross Hands

Photo 23-1

Photo 23-2

Movement 1:

Sink your hips and bend your right leg, shifting your weight toward your right foot. As you turn your body to the right, pivot your left toes inward while angling your right toes slightly outward for better balance. Following the natural turn of your body, parry your right-hand clubbell to the west in an upper horizontal arc just above head height, while warding off with your left-hand clubbell to the east at shoulder height for protection. Keep both elbows slightly bent, with the clubbell heads pointing south in a poised open posture (Photo 23-1).

Movement 2:

Lower your hands in a curved motion from the outside and cross the clubbells in front of your belly with the right-hand clubbell underneath (Photo 23-2).

Movement 3:

Shift your weight onto your left leg and bring your right foot toward your left until both feet are relatively parallel and shoulder-width apart. At the same time, lift the clubbells in front of your chest with rounded arms, allowing the elbows to sink slightly and ward off gently, the right-hand clubbell is still underneath. Maintaining a centered and balanced stance (Photo 23-3).

Photo 23-3

Posture 24: Closing Form

Photo 24-1   Photo 24-2   Photo 24-3

Movement 1:

Extend your arms forward and separate the clubbells to shoulder width with elbows sink slightly (Photo 24-1).

Movement 2:

Lower the clubbells to the front of your hips with the heads still pointing to the south (Photo 24-2).

Movement 3:

Drop the clubbells to the side of your legs, and bring your left foot close to your right foot to finish the form (Photo 24-3).

玉女穿梭
Fair Lady Works with Shuttles

Part III

Tai Chi Cane in Simplified Form 24

Posture 1: Opening Form

Photo 1-1　　　　　　Photo 1-2

Movement 1:

Stand facing the south with your feet shoulder-width apart, toes point relatively forward. Allow your hands to hang naturally down with the cane held horizontally in front of your lower belly. Keep your gaze directed forward (Photo 1-1).

Note: The lines and arrows in Photo 1 indicate the movement paths for the next photo, which is explained in the following paragraph. This pattern continues for all subsequent illustrations.

Movement 2:

Raise your arms forward and upward until the cane reaches shoulder height, keeping arms naturally extended and relaxed, avoid locking your elbows to maintain a sense of fluidity and readiness (Photo 1-2).

Photo 1-3

Movement 3:

Sink your hips and bend your knees slightly, grounding yourself in a stable stance. Lower your elbows and gently press the cane in a horizontal position downward to about hip height. Let the weight of the cane to elastic your arm and drag your shoulder downward, and let your posture convey calmness and stability (Photo 1-3).

Posture 2: Part Wild Horse's Mane

Photo 2-1　　　　Photo 2-2

Movement 1:

Rotate your right hand in a counterclockwise motion to parry the cane tail from your front low to right side, then upward to trace a circular pattern until it rests in front of your chest to guard your centerline. Simultaneously parry your left hand downward in a small arc near your lower belly to cultivate a sense of harmony and balance. Slightly turn your torso to your left, and shift your left foot inward, allowing only the toes to lightly touch the floor for added stability and readiness. At the conclusion of the motion, you are facing the left front corner (southeast), ensuring your body stays grounded and centered (Photo 2-1).

Movement 2:

Step your left foot outward to the left (east), and shift your weight onto your left foot and bend your left knee to form a bow stance. Parry the cane tail from your front centerline diagonally down to your right rib side and lower the handle-hook of the cane to the back side of your right hip. Simultaneously, strike out your left hand to the east at face height. Keep your gaze focused on your left hand (Photo 2-2).

Photo 2-3　　　　　　　　　　　Photo 2-4

Movement 3:

Shift your weight back, lift your left toes, and turn them outward to face the northeast. Then place your entire left foot firmly on the floor. Rotate your body to the left and step your right foot beside your left. At the same time, move your right hand upward and forward to parry the cane tail in a large clockwise circle, deflecting the incoming thread outward to your front right. Then bring the cane tail back toward the front of your chest to maintain protection of your centerline. Simultaneously, rotate your left hand inward in a clockwise circle, drawing it back and lowering it in front of your chest (Photo 2-3).

Movement 4:

Step your right foot forward to the east and shift your weight onto your right foot and bend your right knee to form a bow stance. Simultaneously, strike out the cane tail to your right front corner and parry your left hand to the side of your left hip. Keep your gaze focused on the cane tail end (Photo 2-4).

Photo 2-5　　　　　　　　　　　Photo 2-6

Movement 5:

Shift your weight back, lift your right toes, and turn them outward to face the southeast. Then place your entire right foot on the floor. Rotate your body to the right and step your left foot beside your right. At the same time, rotate your right hand outward to lead the cane tail in a counterclockwise circle, before drawing it back and lowering the cane diagonally in front of your chest. Simultaneously, move your left hand in a circular curve to the front of your abdomen. The cane maintains protection of your centerline (Photo 2-5).

Movement 6:

Step your left foot forward to the east and shift your weight onto your left foot and bend your left knee to form a bow stance. Simultaneously, sweep the cane tail from the front of your chest downward to the back side of your right leg, and strike out your left hand to the east at face height. Keep your gaze focused on your left hand (Photo 2-6).

Posture 3: White Crane Spreading Its Wings

Photo 3-1   Photo 3-2

Movement 1:

Step your right foot half a step closer to your left foot while slightly turning your torso to the left. Parry your left hand to the front of your right shoulder, and sweep the cane tail from the back side of your right leg to the front of your left leg. This forms a diagonal protection of your front centerline (Photo 3-1).

Movement 2:

Move your left foot slightly backward, placing only the toes on the floor to form a left empty stance. Simultaneously, circle up your right hand from the front of your chest and go through the outside of your left shoulder and end it above your head. The cane serves a large parry motion from your front low to front high as if to deflect an attack off your centerline. At the same time, drop your left palm under your right armpit (Photo 3-2).

Photo 3-3   Photo 3-4

Movement 3:

Wrap the cane from the outside of your left shoulder, passing it behind your back, and strike with the cane tail from the outside of your right shoulder across the front of your body, ending in front of your left shoulder. Your right hand moves the cane handle downward from above your head to the front of your right abdomen. At the same time, move your left palm in front of your left shoulder, with the palm facing the cane tail section (Photo 3-3).

Movement 4:

Move your left foot slightly forward, placing only the toes on the floor to form a left empty stance. Strike the cane tail upward to the front right with your right hand, while your left hand parries in a curved path to the side of your left hip. Keep both arms softly rounded. Your body is relatively facing east (Photo 3-4).

Posture 4: Brush Knee on Both Sides

Photo 4-1

Photo 4-2

Movement 1:

Parry the cane tail in a downward arc, guided by the twisting of your torso to the left. This motion leads your right hand to bring the cane from above the front of your head down to the front of your chest, as if deflecting an incoming strike to your face. At the same time, arc your left hand upward and inward from the side of your left hip to the front of your face, forming a closed defensive posture. Your left hand positions behind the cane tail for added protection (Photo 4-1).

Movement 2:

Without pausing, rotate your torso to the right, as if releasing a twisted spring from the previous leftward motion. This rotation powers the cane into a parrying action toward your right side, with the cane angled diagonally in front of your chest. Your left palm supports the lower part of the cane at upper chest height, while your right hand holds the handle-hook in front of your abdomen (Photo 4-2).

Photo 4-3

Movement 3:

Step forward with your left foot to the east into a left bow stance. Simultaneously, move your left hand in a downward arc, follow your torso turning to the left to parry the lower part of the cane from the front of your chest to the front of your left hip. This movement creates a "brush away" motion to deflect an incoming attack to your chest. At the same time, circle your right hand to move the cane handle-hook upward from the rear right corner, above your right shoulder, and strike it forward to the east at face height. As you strike the handle-hook, you can slide your right hand toward the middle point of the cane to extend the reach of the forward motion. Sink your right shoulder and keep your right elbow slightly down (Photo 4-3).

Photo 4-4   Photo 4-4R

Photo 4-5

Movement 4:

Shift your weight back slightly to raise the toes of your left foot, turning your torso a bit to the left. Then, move up your right foot to the side of your left foot with the ball touching the floor. At the same time, move the cane handle-hook backward toward your chest to protect your centerline, and follow your torso's leftward twist to parry it to your left side. Maintain the cane diagonally in front of your left hip and right shoulder (Photo 4-4 and 4-4R).

Movement 5:

Step forward with your right foot to the east into a right bow stance. At the same time, move your right hand in a downward arc, following the rotation of your torso to the right, and parry the cane handle-hook to the front of your right hip. Simultaneously, circle your left hand to lift the cane tail upward from the rear left corner, bringing it above your left shoulder, and strike it forward to the east at face height. As you deliver the strike, slide your left hand toward the midpoint of the cane and your right hand toward the end of the handle-hook to extend the reach of the forward motion. Keep your left shoulder relaxed and your left elbow slightly lowered (Photo 4-5).

Photo 4-6   Photo 4-7

Movement 6:

Repeat Movement 2 & 3 (Photo 4-6, 4-7).

Posture 5: Playing a Guitar

Photo 5-1   Photo 5-2

Movement 1:

Step your right foot half a step closer to your left heel. At the same time, withdraw your right hand to parry the handle-hook outward toward the outside of your right shoulder, while bringing your left hand slightly forward in front of your left abdomen. At the end of the movement, both hands hold the cane diagonally across your chest, forming a closing and protective posture (Photo 5-1).

Movement 2:

Step your left foot slightly forward to the east, placing the heel on the floor with the toes raised and the knee slightly bent to form a left empty stance. At the same time, extend the cane tail end forward and upward to face height, while twisting the handle-hook downward and inward to the front of your abdomen. Sink both hips, lengthen your spine, lift your head, and keep your shoulders and elbows relaxed and lowered (Photo 5-2).

Posture 6: Repulse Monkey

Photo 6-1　　　　　　　　　Photo 6-2

Movement 1:

Turn your torso slightly to the right and draw your left foot back slightly, placing the toes on the floor. Sweep the cane from in front of you downward and backward, passing along the side of your right leg to the rear right corner, ending at shoulder height. At the same time, extend your left hand slightly forward with the palm facing upward. At the end of the motion, both arms should be opened wide with elbows slightly bent. First, glance at your right hand as it moves back, then shift your gaze to your left palm in front of you (Photo 6-1).

Movement 2:

Rotate your torso to the left while stepping your left foot back and turning the heel of your right foot outward. At the same time, bend your right arm and bring the cane past your right ear before striking it forward in front of your chest. Simultaneously, parry your left hand in a downward curve toward your left abdomen (Photo 6-2).

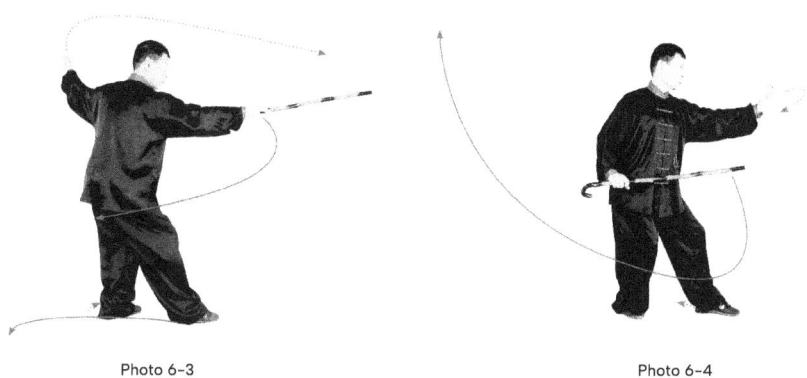

Photo 6-3   Photo 6-4

Movement 3:

Move your left hand in a backward arc past the outside of your left hip, rising to shoulder height toward your left rear corner. At the same time, extend the cane tail forward to the east and slightly parry it outward, forming an open-arms posture with both elbows slightly bent. First, glance at your left palm as it arcs back, then shift your gaze to the cane tail in front of you (Photo 6-3).

Movement 4:

Step your right foot back while twisting the heel of your left foot outward to avoid straining your left knee. At the same time, parry the cane downward with your right hand, drawing the handle-hook back to the side of your right hip so the cane tail guard is positioned in front of your right abdomen. Simultaneously, bend your left arm past your left ear, then strike your left palm forward in front of your chest (Photo 6-4).

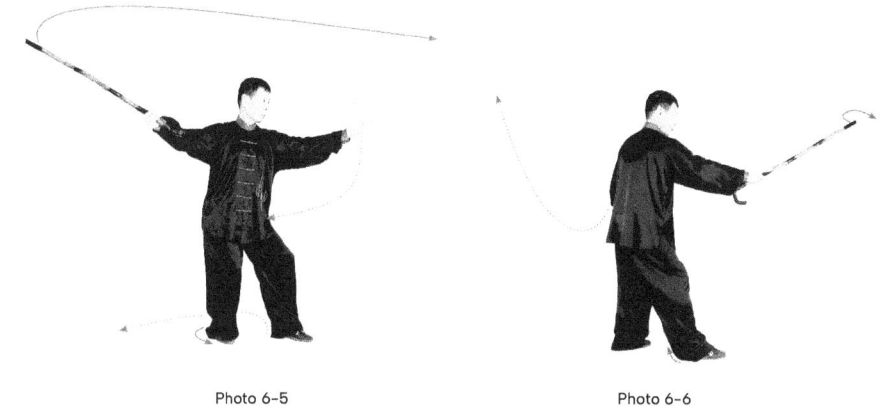

Photo 6-5   Photo 6-6

Movement 5:

Repeat Movement 1 and 2 (Photo 6-5 and 6-6).

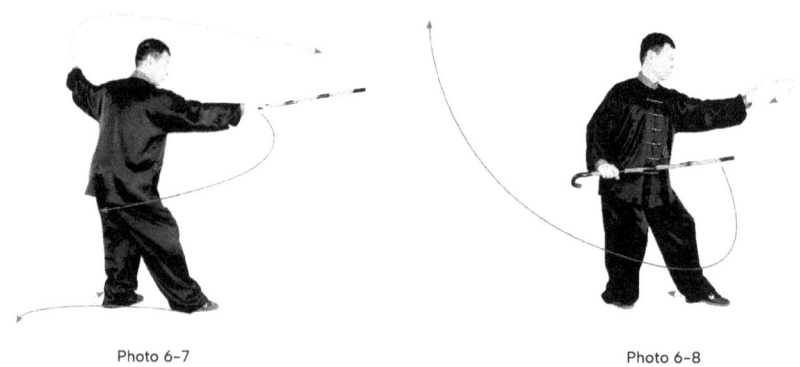

Photo 6-7   Photo 6-8

Movement 6:

Repeat Movement 3 and 4 (Photo 6-7 and 6-8).

Photo 6-9

Movement 7:

Repeat Movement 1 (Photo 6-9).

Posture 7: Grasp the Bird's Tail - Left

Photo 7-1 Photo 7-2

Movement 1:

Withdraw your left foot a bit toward your right, lightly touching the floor with the ball of the left foot to form a left empty stance. At the same time, raise your right hand, tilting the cane's tail downward beside your right shoulder. Circle the cane behind your back from right to left, ending near your left shoulder as if shielding the back of your head from an attack. Then lower your right hand in front of your chest, holding the cane horizontally, while your left hand moves downward and inward to the front of your belly (Photo 7-1).

Movement 2:

Slide your left forearm and hand over the cane to grasp it with your left hand. Step your left foot forward to the east into a left bow stance, bending the knee. At the same time, parry your right hand downward toward your right hip, while lifting the cane with your left hand upward and forward in front of your chest, as if warding off an incoming force. Keep both arms rounded and coordinate the step and parry smoothly (Photo 7-2).

Photo 7-3 Photo 7-4

Movement 3:

Turn your torso slightly to the left as you extend the cane's handle hook slightly forward to the east. At the same time, circle your left arm clockwise and grasp the cane's tail with your right hand, twisting it from the outside of your left shoulder to the front of your chest. The cane should now be held diagonally, pointing east, with the handle hook at face height and the tail near your abdomen (Photo 7-3).

Movement 4:

Without pausing, turn your torso slightly to the right while pulling the cane with both hands in a backward and downward curved motion, applying plucking-down energy. End with the cane nearly parallel to the floor as you shift your weight back onto your right foot (Photo 7-4).

Photo 7-5 Photo 7-6

Movement 5:

Turn your torso to the left to face east, simultaneously drawing your left hand back and pushing your right hand forward to hold the cane horizontally in front of your chest. Then, twist the cane counterclockwise, folding your right forearm over your left. The cane handle hook is at your right elbow head side. As you do this, shift your weight forward onto your left leg, settling into a left bow stance. Keep your gaze focused toward the east, expressing the intent and energy of a forward press (Photo 7-5).

Movement 6:

Unfold your arms and rotate the cane in a full clockwise circle, switching your grip so that your right hand holds near the handle hook and your left hand grips near the tail end. Remain in the left bow stance. Both palms face downward as you hold the cane horizontally in front of your chest, with arms slightly extended (Photo 7-6).

Photo 7-7　　　　　　　　　　Photo 7-8

Movement 7:

Gradually shift your weight back onto your right leg, lifting the toes of your left foot slightly to support the transition. At the same time, draw both hands back and parry the cane upward in a smooth curve to the front of your forehead, forming a horizontal protective position (Photo 7-7).

Movement 8:

Shift your weight forward onto your left leg and pivot your right heel backward, settling into a stable left bow stance. At the same time, lower the cane in front of your chest, then push it forward and upward with both arms extended—elbows slightly bent and relaxed. Keep your gaze directed straight ahead to the east, maintaining balance and projecting clear focus and intent (Photo 7-8).

Posture 8: Grasp the Bird's Tail - Right

Photo 8-1   Photo 8-2

Movement 1:

Shift your weight onto your right leg as you gently turn your torso to the right. At the same time, strike the cane's handle hook toward the west in a slightly upward arc, as if parrying an incoming force. Simultaneously, turn the toes of your left foot a bit inward, and the toes of your right foot outward to protect your knees from strain. Maintain your arms in a rounded shape to hold the cane in a warding-off position, Focus on coordinating your torso and arm movements fluidly while grounding your stance (Photo 8-1).

Movement 2:

Turn the toes of your left foot inward as you rotate slightly to the right. Then, shift your weight onto your left foot, and bring your right foot beside your left, with the ball of your right foot lightly touching the floor to form a right empty stance. At the same time, tilt the cane with the handle hook upward and the tail downward, parrying the cane diagonally in front of you to protect your face and chest, while moving your left hand to the right side of your ribs. This posture symbolizes a closing defensive pose, embodying readiness, control, balance, and focus (Photo 8-2).

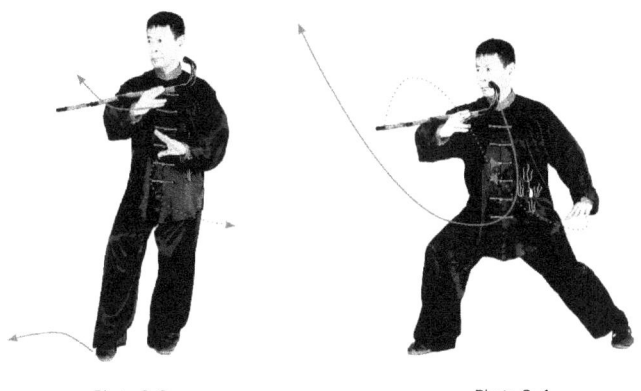

Photo 8-3   Photo 8-4

Movement 3:

Wrap the cane from the outside of your left shoulder across the back of your head to the back of your right shoulder. Then, lower the handle hook and bend your right forearm to guide the handle end in front of your left chest, holding the cane horizontally across your upper chest. At the same time, circle your left hand downward, outward, then upward and inward, bringing it to rest a few inches beneath your right hand (Photo 8-3).

Movement 4:

Step your right foot forward to the west into a left bow stance, bending the knee. At the same time, parry your left hand downward toward the outside of your left hip, while moving the cane with your right hand forward in front of your chest, as if warding off an incoming force. Keep both arms rounded and coordinate the step and parry smoothly (Photo 8-4)

Photo 8-5   Photo 8-6

Photo 8-7 Photo 8-8

Photo 8-9 Photo 8-10

Movement 5:

Repeat the Movement 3, 4, 5, 6, 7, and 8 in Posture 7: Grasp the Bird's Tail - Left, and reversing "left" and "right" (Photo 8-5, 8-6, 8-7, 8-8, 8-9, and 8-10).

Posture 9: Single Whip

Photo 9-1

Photo 9-2

Movement 1:

Sink your right hip and shift your weight onto your left foot while turning your right toes inward. At the same time, rotate your torso to the left and parry the cane's handle slightly upward toward the outside of your left shoulder to guard. Then, turn your left toes outward to protect your left knee from strain (Photo 9-1).

Movement 2:

Turn your torso slightly further to the left and turn your right toes inward again (you may need to step your right foot slightly closer to your left foot to narrow the stance). At the same time, paddle the cane's tail end downward to guard in front of your right knee. Direct your gaze toward your left side (Photo 9-2).

Photo 9-3   Photo 9-4

Movement 3:

Continue turning your torso to the left as you paddle the cane's tail upward, maintaining a circular motion from the front of your right knee to the front of your left shoulder. Then, parry the cane in a U-turn back toward the front of your right shoulder by twisting your torso back to the right. At the end of the movement, your left hand and the cane handle should be positioned in front of your abdomen, with your right hand holding the middle section of the cane, palm facing outward. The cane should now be in a relatively vertical position (Photo 9-3).

Movement 4:

Without pausing, twist your torso slightly back to the left to guide the cane in a counterclockwise curve to your left. Then, twist your torso back to your right to paddle the cane's tail downward across your abdomen as if clearing away an attack. At the same time, raise your left hand, positioning the handle hook to guard the front of your upper chest. Keep your gaze directed to your left side (Photo 9-4).

Photo 9-5

Movement 5:

Turn your torso to the left and step your left foot forward to the east, settling into a strong and balanced left bow stance. At the same time, whip the cane in a striking motion from your right rib side across your face to the left at shoulder height. Following the leftward motion, execute a controlled parry with your right hand toward the southwest corner, gathering the five fingers together to form a hook-hand. This maintains counterbalance and structural integrity with the movement of the left hand (Photo 9-5).

Posture 10: Wave Hands Like Clouds

Photo 10-1

Photo 10-2

Movement 1:

Sink your right hip and gradually shift your weight onto your right foot while simultaneously turning your torso toward the right front corner and turning your left toes slightly inward. At the same time, parry the cane from the left through a downward curve across the front of your abdomen, then toss it to your right hand. Catch the cane near the handle with your right hand, holding it relatively vertically, warding off toward your right front corner with the cane's tail pointing upward (Photo 10-1).

Movement 2:

Tilt the cane's tail downward by twisting your right wrist in a clockwise motion, turning the palm outward with the thumb pointing downward. At the same time, draw your right foot closer to your left leg and bring in your left hand to support the cane handle, assisting in parrying the cane's tail outside of your right leg (Photo 10-2).

Photo 10-3

Photo 10-4

Movement 3:

Twist your torso slightly further to the right to parry the cane from the outside (west) of your right leg toward your right rear corner (northwest), spinning the cane's tail upward. Then, twist your torso back toward your front right (southwest). Your stance remains unchanged, with only the hip and waist twisting to drive the motion (Photo 10-3). Throughout movements 1 to 3, the cane's tail traces a diagonally vertical circle, clearing the space from your right front, sweeping low toward your right rear, and returning to your right front. The movement is powered entirely by the twisting of your torso, as if winding a spring to generate torque that drives the spine of the cane.

Movement 4:

Without pausing, slide your left hand from above the handle down to the middle of the cane, and paddle the cane's tail downward again as if deflecting an incoming attack toward your right chest. At the end of the motion, the cane stands vertically, guarding your right front, with the tail positioned at the side of your right knee and the handle hook aligned with your right ear (Photo 10-4).

Photo 10-5 Photo 10-6

Movement 5:

Continue to spin the cane, sweeping the tail across the outside of your right leg, through your right rear, and upward to position it behind your right shoulder. Release your left hand from the cane, positioning it with the palm facing your right rib side. Your right hand holds the cane near the handle hook at the side of your right hip, with fingertips pointing relatively to the floor. Keep your gaze directed toward your left side (Photo 10-5).

Movement 6:

Turn your torso slightly to the left and twist the cane out from behind your right arm using your right wrist. Spin the cane in a clockwise circle and finish with both hands gripping near the handle hook, as if holding a baseball bat vertically in front of your right shoulder. At the same time, move your right foot slightly closer to your left foot (Photo 10-6).

Photo 10-7   Photo 10-8

Movement 7:

Twist your torso to the left and sling the cane's tail from your right front corner (southwest) across your lower front to your left rear upper corner (northeast). At the same time, adjust your feet so that both toes point toward the east to prevent strain on your knees. This movement is a larger, more forceful swing to strike outward with the cane (Photo 10-7).

Movement 8:

Coil the cane in a counterclockwise circle, parrying the cane's tail from the upper northeast to the lower southeast corner, with your hands holding near the handle hook at face height. Simultaneously, twist your right heel inward and turn your left toes inward, aligning your feet relatively parallel with toes pointing south. This is a defensive pose with the cane protesting your head and upper chest (Photo 10-8).

Photo 10-9   Photo 10-10

Movement 9:

Turn your torso to the right and release your left hand from the cane. Swing the cane with your right hand in a large upward curve, moving from your left front, across the front of your head, to your right front, with the cane's tail high in front of your head and the handle positioned in front of your right abdomen. At the same time, step your left foot toward the east and turn your right toes slightly outward toward the right front corner. Your left hand parries downward to the front of your abdomen (Photo 10-9).

Movement 10:

Repeat Movement 2 (Photo 10-10).

Photo 10-11   Photo 10-12

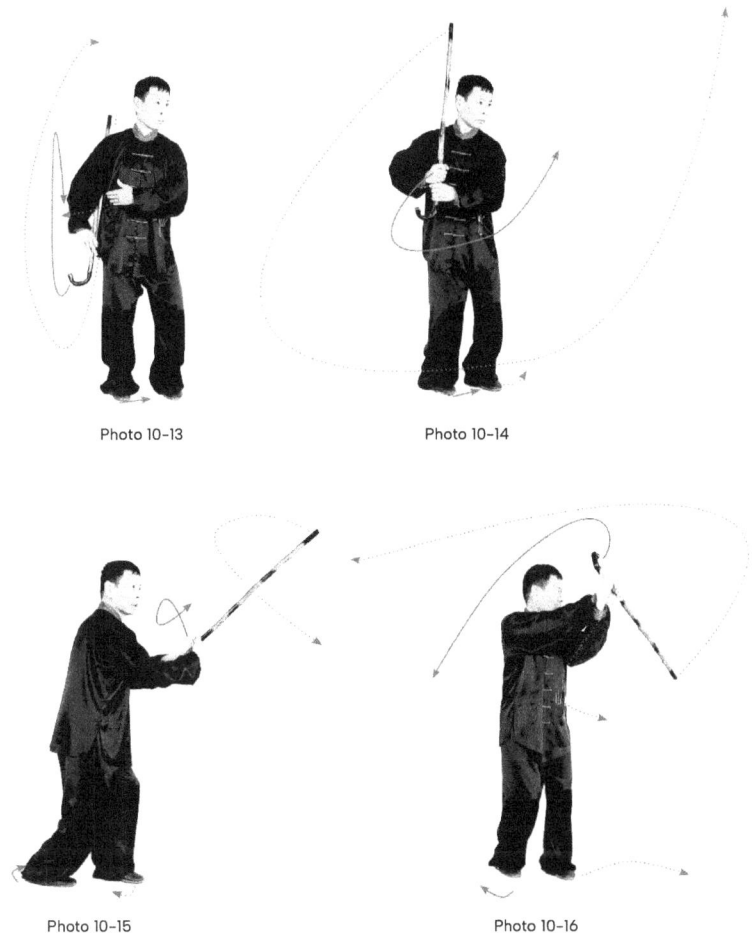

Photo 10-13 Photo 10-14

Photo 10-15 Photo 10-16

Movement 11:

Repeat Movements 3 through 8 for the second step of Wave Hands Like Clouds. As you flow through these motions, allow the cane to circle smoothly around your body, guiding its energy with your torso's rotation and coordinated footwork (Photo 10-11, 10-12, 10-13, 10-14, 10-15, 10-16).

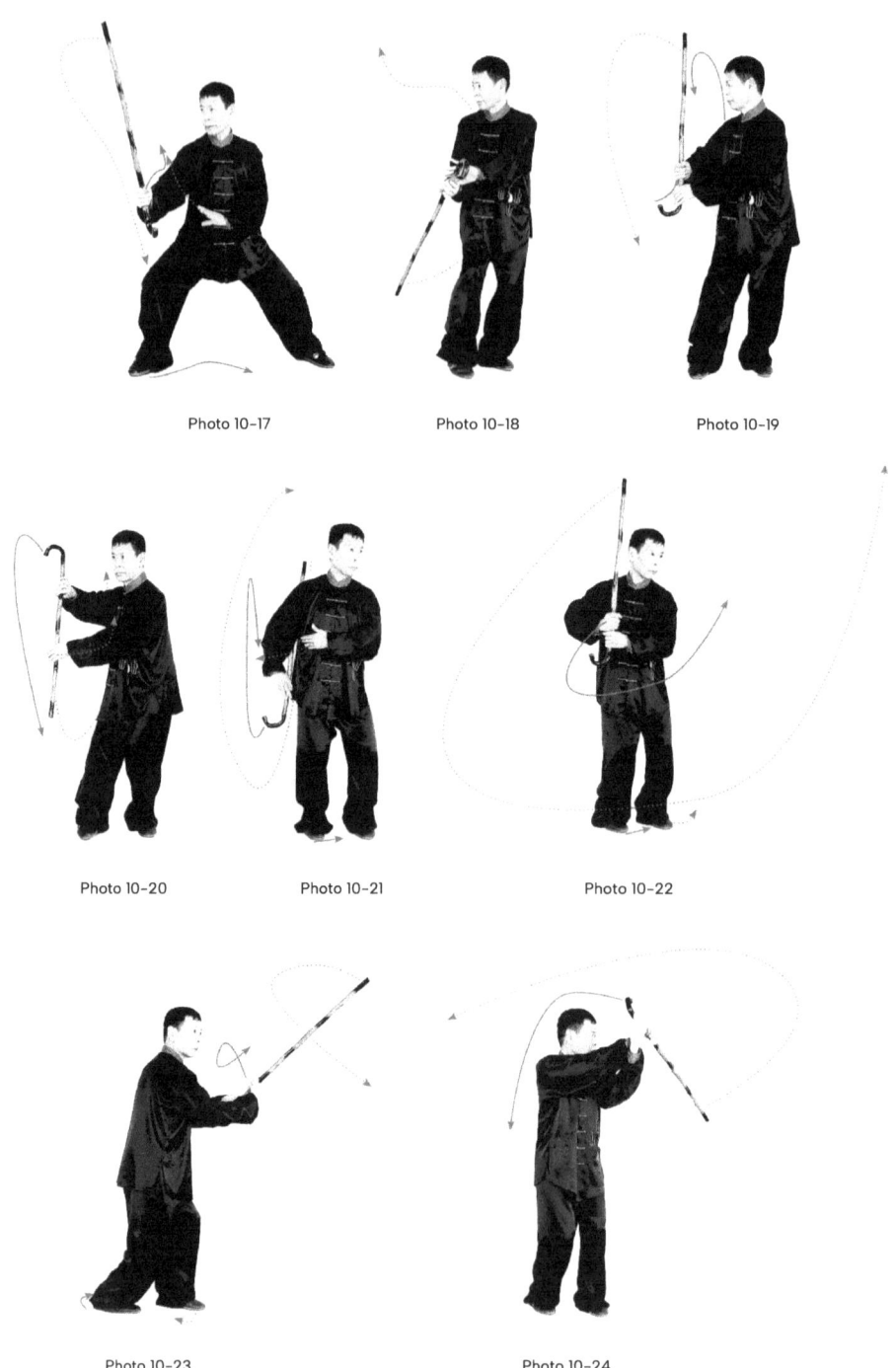

Photo 10-17

Photo 10-18

Photo 10-19

Photo 10-20

Photo 10-21

Photo 10-22

Photo 10-23

Photo 10-24

Movement 12:

Repeat Movements 9, 10, and 3 through 8 another cycle for the third step of the "Wave Hands Like Clouds" sequence. With each cycle, step gradually toward the east, totally advancing with three steady steps. Maintain a calm and rooted demeanor as the cane traces elegant arcs through space, embodying both defense and fluid power. This sequence culminates in a harmonious blend of movement and intention, with the cane seamlessly weaving around your form in rhythmic waves (Photo 10-17, 10-18, 10-19, 10-20, 10-21, 10-22, 10-23, 10-24).

Posture 11: Single Whip

Photo 11-1

Photo 11-2

Movement 1:

Turn your torso to the right and swing the cane with both hands in a large upward curve, moving from your left front, across the front of your head, to your right front, with the cane's tail held high in front of your head and the handle positioned near your right abdomen. Keep your gaze directed toward your right front corner (Photo 11-1).

Movement 2:

Tilt the cane's tail downward by twisting and bending your right wrist in a clockwise motion, turning the palm outward with the thumb side underneath. At the same time, use your left hand to support the cane handle, assisting in parrying the cane's tail outside of your right leg (Photo 11-2).

Photo 11-.3   Photo 11-4

Movement 3:

Use the twisting of your torso toward your right rear to paddle the cane from the outside of your right knee across your back. At the same time, lift the cane handle up behind your head to position the cane's tail over the back of your left shoulder. Simultaneously, drop your left palm under your right armpit and move your left foot slightly closer to your right foot, with the toes lightly touching the floor. Keep your gaze directed toward the east (Photo 11-3).

Movement 4:

Step your left foot forward to the east into a strong and balanced left bow stance. At the same time, whip the cane from the outside of your left shoulder across your chest toward the southwest corner, while striking with your left hand from your right rib side across your face to the left at shoulder height. The large, open motion of your extended left palm and cane maintains counterbalance and structural integrity within the form (Photo 11-4).

Posture 12: High Pat on Horse

Photo 12-1   Photo 12-2

Movement 1:

Step your right foot forward by half a step, bringing it closer to your left foot, then smoothly shift your weight onto your right leg to form a left empty stance. Simultaneously, bend your right arm and parry the cane forward to the front of your chest with the cane's tail pointing to your left side (north). As you make this transition, turn your left palm facing up and bring it a bit back. Hold the cane horizontally in front of your chest to maintain a protective pose toward the east (Photo 12-1).

Movement 2:

Strike the cane forward with your right arm lined up with the cane with the cane tail pointing to the east. At the same time, parry your left hand in a smooth downward curve toward the front of your left hip, creating a harmonious and balanced motion with the cane striking out. Lift up your left heel a bit to straighten up your torso (Photo 12-2).

Posture 13: Kick with Right Heel

Photo 13-1   Photo 13-2

Movement 1:

Deflect the cane in a clockwise circle to clear the space in front of your face and above your head. Then, round your right arm to hold the cane horizontally in front of your chest. Raise your left palm to support the cane near the handle, keeping both arms rounded to create a shield-like protective structure in front of you. Simultaneously, lift your left knee to prepare for the next step. Hold this balanced stance briefly, ensuring stability and control before transitioning (Photo 13-1).

Movement 2:

Step your left foot forward toward the northeast and settle into a strong, rooted left bow stance. At the same time, parry your left palm to the left front while moving the cane handle with your right hand to the right front, as if redirecting an incoming force. Maintain the warding-off energy by keeping both arms rounded (Photo 13-2).

Photo 13-3   Photo 13-4

Movement 3:

Continue the fluid motion of your hands in a downward-then-upward curve until they cross again in front of your chest, with your right hand holding the cane on the outside. Keep your arms rounded, forming a shield-like ward-off structure. Simultaneously, lift your right knee up to abdomen height, balancing on your left leg in a stable left-leg rooster stance, with your right toes pointing diagonally downward. Engage your core to maintain balance and stability in this poised position (Photo 13-3).

Movement 4:

Separate your hands sideways to shoulder height, keeping your elbows slightly bent. At the same time, execute a right front kick toward the southeast corner, maintaining your gaze on your right foot. Deliver the kicking force through the right heel. Coordinate your arm movements with the kick: your right arm remains above and parallel to your right leg, while your left arm and palm extend slightly toward the northwest corner. Maintain balance and control throughout this dynamic movement (Photo 13-4).

Posture 14: Strike Opponent's Ears with Both Fists

Photo 14-1　　　　　　　　Photo 14-2

Movement 1:

Pull back your right leg before placing it down toward the southeast corner in a controlled landing, adjusting your left heel slightly outward to align your chest facing the southeast. As you do so, parry the cane's tail in a smooth counterclockwise circle to clear the space in front of your face, then sweep it downward in front of your abdomen. Simultaneously, move your left hand inward to grasp the cane near the tail end. Hold the cane horizontally in front of your abdomen, forming a protective ward-off posture. Keep your focus toward your right front corner, maintaining stability and awareness in your stance (Photo 14-1).

Movement 2:

Shift your weight forward onto your right leg, transitioning into a strong right bow stance. At the same time, strike the cane upward and forward with both hands to reach eye height. Maintain proper structure by keeping your shoulders relaxed, elbows slightly lowered, and arms rounded to effectively channel strength while preserving the integrity of the movement (Photo 14-2).

Posture 15: Kick with Left Heel

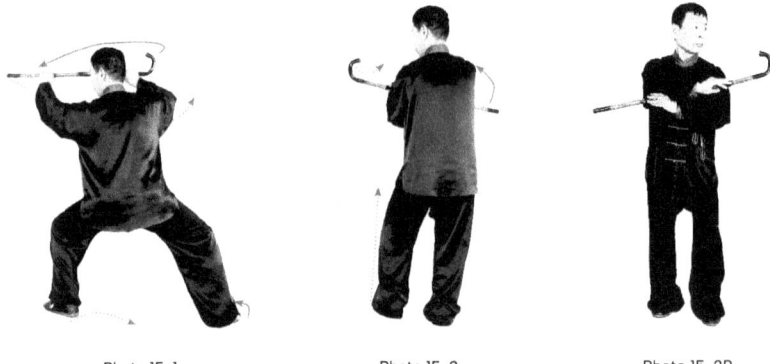

Photo 15-1 Photo 15-2 Photo 15-2R

Movement 1:

Sink your hips and turn your torso to the left, striking the cane's tail toward the northwest corner while drawing your left heel inward and turning your right toes slightly inward to adjust your stance. Maintain a rounded structure with both arms, keeping the elbows slightly sunk to sustain a balanced ward-off energy (Photo 15-1).

Movement 2:

Turn your torso slightly further to the left and turn your right toes a bit more inward. At the same time, fold the cane counterclockwise, positioning your right hand on top of your left forearm, with the cane's handle hook resting above and outside your left elbow. This creates a protective, shield-like structure with the cane between your rounded arms. Simultaneously, shift your weight onto your right leg and move your left foot halfway toward your right foot, with the toes lightly touching the floor (Photos. 15-2 & 15-2R).

Photo 15-3 Photo 15-4

Movement 3:

Lift your left foot, raising the knee to abdomen height. Maintain a steady rooster stance, balancing on your right foot, and direct your gaze toward the northwest corner (Photo 15-3).

Movement 4:

Separate your hands sideways to shoulder height, keeping the elbows slightly bent. At the same time, execute a left heel kick toward the northwest corner. Coordinate the arm movements with the kick: your left arm holding the cane stays above and parallel to your left leg, while your right arm and palm extend slightly toward the southeast corner. Maintain balance, structure, and control throughout this dynamic movement (Photo 15-4).

Posture 16: Golden Rooster Stands on One Leg - Left

Photo 16-1　　　　　　Photo 16-2

Movement 1:

Draw your left foot inward close to your right leg, either lightly touching the floor for balance or keeping it lifted if your stability allows. At the same time, parry the cane from your left front across your abdomen to the front of your right shoulder, and grasp the cane with your right hand near the handle. Hold the cane vertically, warding off toward the northeast corner (Photo 16-1).

Movement 2:

Lower your weight onto your right foot, then step your left foot backward toward the west at a slight angle to the southwest. Bend your right knee into a right bow stance while pushing the vertical cane slightly outward to balance the extension of your left leg (Photo 16-2).

Photo 16-3　　　　　　Photo 16-3 easy

Photo 16-4

Movement 3:

Bend your right knee into a deep crouch while turning your head to the west, and angle your left foot slightly outward toward the northwest. This position is called pu-bu, a lower stance in Tai Chi practice. If flexibility is limited, you may simplify it into a partial horse stance (see Photo 16-3 easy). At the same time, press the cane downward with its tail along the inner side of your left thigh. Keep your weight centered over your right heel, maintaining a slight arch in your left knee for joint protection (Photo 16-3).

Movement 4:

Rise from the low form by shifting your weight onto your left foot and straightening your right leg. Pivot your right toes inward while bending your left knee into a stable left bow stance. At the same time, strike the cane's tail westward at chest height (Photo 16-4).

Photo 16-5   Photo 16-6

Movement 5:

Step your right foot slightly forward in front of your left foot, maintaining balance and stability. At the same time, parry the cane in a full vertical circle along the right side of your torso—moving upward, backward, downward, forward and upward again—ending with the cane held vertically in front of your right shoulder. Be sure to flex your right wrist to facilitate the cane's smooth circular motion (Photo 16-5).

Movement 6:

Raise your right knee in front of your torso, maintaining balance and stability. Simultaneously, parry the cane forward and slightly upward, positioning it in front of your right shoulder for protection. Meanwhile, press your left palm downward beside your left hip. This iconic posture, known as the Golden Rooster Stands on One Leg, embodies balance, focus, and inner strength (Photo 16-6).

Posture 17: Golden Rooster Stands on One Leg - Right

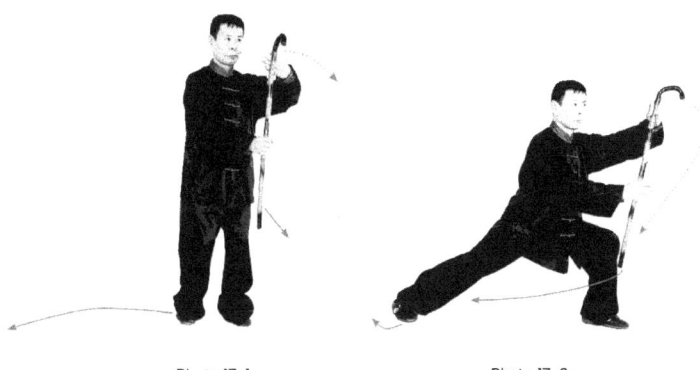

Photo 17-1   Photo 17-2

Movement 1:

Lower your right foot, placing the ball of your foot on the floor a bit in front of your left foot. Simultaneously, turn your torso to the left and pivot your left heel inward to protect your left knee from strain, while parrying the cane's tail in a downward and inward curve toward your left front side. At the same time, toss (or hand) the cane to your left hand, with your left hand grasping near the handle hook and your right hand holding the middle section of the cane (Photo 17-1).

Movement 2:

Repeat Movements 2, 3, 4, 5, and 6 from Posture 16: Left Lower Form and Stand on One Leg, reversing the facing direction as well as the left and right hands (Photos. 17-2, 17-3, 17-3 easy, 17-4, 17-5 and 17-6).

Photo 17-3   Photo 17-3 easy

Photo 17-4

Photo 17-5

Photo 17-6

Posture 18: Fair Lady Works with Shuttles on Both Sides

Photo 18-1   Photo 18-2

Movement 1:

Step your left foot forward with the toes pointing outward toward the southwest corner. As you do so, parry the cane in a counterclockwise outward curve, then bring the cane's tail back in front of your left chest. Simultaneously, shift your weight onto your left foot while drawing your right hand in an inward circle toward your lower abdomen, forming a protective posture centered in front of your torso (Photo 18-1).

Movement 2:

Step your right foot closer to the left, lightly touching the ground with your right toes. Take the cane from your left hand, grasping the middle section with your right hand. Extend your right hand toward your right front (northwest), holding the cane horizontally at shoulder height to ward off. At the same time, sweep your left hand in a smooth downward arc to the side of your left ribs (Photo 18-2).

Movement 3:

Without pausing, shift your weight onto your right leg and settle into a right bow stance. Simultaneously, raise the cane horizontally above your head and push your left palm upward and forward in front of your chest, directing both toward the northwest corner (Photo 18-3).

Photo 18-3

Photo 18-4　　　Photo 18-5

Movement 4:

Turn your right foot slightly outward to adjust your balance, and draw your left foot in beside your right, with only the toes lightly touching the floor. At the same time, twist your torso slightly to the left and parry the cane's handle hook from above your head downward toward the front of your left hip. Let your left hand assist in guiding and controlling the cane (Photo 18-4).

Movement 5:

Maintaining the same stance, twist your torso to the right and spin the cane in a clockwise circle, guiding the handle from in front of your left hip, across your chest, and down to the front of your right hip (Photo 18-5).

Photo 18-6　　　Photo 18-7

Movement 6:

Maintaining the same stance, twist your torso to the left and spin the cane in a counterclockwise circle, guiding the handle from in front of your right hip, across your chest, and down to the front of your left hip (Photo 18-6).

Movement 7:

Repeat Movement 5 exactly the same (Photo 18-7).

Movement 8:

Release your right hand from the cane and hold it with your left hand at the middle section. Parry the cane from the front of your right abdomen across your chest to your left front (southwest) corner at shoulder height. Drop your right hand to your right rib side. At the same time, lift your left heel and draw it inward, placing only the toes on the floor to form a left empty stance. Gaze toward the southwest (Photo 18-8).

Movement 9:

Without pausing, step your left foot toward the southwest and shift your weight onto your left leg, settling into a left bow stance. Simultaneously, raise the cane horizontally above your head with your left hand, and push your right palm upward and forward in front of your chest, both directed toward the southwest corner (Photo 18-9).

Posture 19: Needle at Sea Bottom

Photo 19-1　　　　　　　　　Photo 19-2

Movement 1:

Step your right foot forward by half a step and shift your weight onto it. At the same time, turn your torso slightly to the right while parrying the cane downward from above your head to the front of your chest. Then, use your right hand to grasp the cane near the handle. Hold the cane with both hands horizontally in front of your chest as a protective guard (Photo 19-1).

Movement 2:

Release your left hand from the cane and guide the cane's tail diagonally downward toward the front of your right knee. Simultaneously, parry your left palm upward to the front of your right shoulder. Move your left foot slightly forward, keeping only the ball of the foot touching the floor to form a left empty stance (Photo 19-2).

Photo 19-3　　　　　　　　　Photo 19-4

Movement 3:

Turn your torso slightly to the right and sweep the cane's tail from the front of your right knee toward your right rear corner (northeast). At the same time, parry your left palm to the front of your left abdomen, maintaining a balanced and alert posture (Photo 19-3).

Movement 4:

Step your left foot slightly forward, keeping only the toes touching the floor, and hinge forward at the hips. As you do so, strike the cane's tail downward and forward to the west, while parrying your left hand downward and outward near the side of your left knee to support balance and provide additional protection (Photo 19-4).

Posture 20: Fan Through the Back

Photo 20-1   Photo 20-2

Movement 1:

Straighten your torso as you draw your left foot back toward your right, keeping the toes lightly touching the floor. At the same time, parry the cane's tail in a small counterclockwise circle, then lift it in front of your chest, pointing toward the west. Simultaneously, raise your left hand and position it just beneath your right wrist, both hands aligned in front of your chest (Photo 20-1).

Movement 2:

Without pausing, turn your torso slightly to the right as you step your left foot forward toward the west, shifting your weight onto it and settling into a stable left bow stance. As you do so, parry the cane upward and backward to the outside of your right temple, while pushing your left palm forward at shoulder height toward the west (Photo 20-2).

Posture 21: Turn to Deflect, Parry and Punch

Photo 21-1　　　　Photo 21-2　　　　Photo 21-2 easy

Movement 1:

Shift your weight temporarily onto your right foot and turn your torso to the right, rotating your orientation from facing west to facing east. Simultaneously, turn your left toes inward. Then, shift your weight back onto your left foot and draw your right foot close, keeping only the ball of the foot touching the floor in a right empty stance. As you do so, sweep the cane in a rightward arc downward in front of your right knee, while moving your left hand across your head to position it in front of your right shoulder (Photo 21-1).

Movement 2:

Continue rotating your torso to the right and step your right foot slightly out toward the east, angling the toes diagonally toward the southeast. At the same time, pivot your left heel outward to assist the torso twist and lower into a *xie-bu* (resting stance). Simultaneously, deflect the cane in a clockwise arc toward the southeast. If flexibility is limited, this movement can be simplified into a high crossing stance (Photo 21-2 & 21-2 easy).

Photo 21-3　　　　Photo 21-4

Movement 3:

Rise to standing and step your left foot forward toward the east, keeping most of your weight on your right leg. At the same time, parry your left hand upward in front of your chest, and bring the cane close to your right rib cage with the cane's tail pointing to the east (Photo 21-3).

Movement 4:

Shift your weight onto your left foot and slightly draw your right heel back to settle into a stable left bow stance. Simultaneously, strike the cane's tail upward and forward toward the east at upper chest height. Keep your right elbow slightly bent to maintain structural integrity and control, while your left hand draws back to support the cane's handle hook. For greater striking power, you may step your left foot slightly farther forward to help generate forward momentum (Photo 21-4).

Posture 22: Apparent Closure

Photo 22-1 Photo 22-2

Movement 1:

Coil the cane in a counterclockwise vertical circle in front of your face, turning the cane's tail to point north. Then, hold the cane horizontally in front of your chest with both hands to create a ward-off protective posture (Photo 22-1).

Movement 2:

Shift your weight back onto your right leg, lifting the toes of your left foot slightly off the floor. Simultaneously, raise the cane in front of your face and follow the backward body shift by rolling the cane horizontally above your head (Photo 22-2).

Movement 3:

Press the cane downward in front of your chest, then push it upward toward the east until it reaches shoulder height. As you do this, shift your weight forward by pressing down your left toes and bending your left knee, settling into a stable left bow stance. Keep your shoulders relaxed, elbows slightly sunken, and arms warded off outward to maintain a balanced and powerful posture (Photo 22-3).

Photo 22-3

Posture 23: Cross Hands

Photo 23-1

Photo 23-2

Movement 1:

Sink your hips and bend your right knee, turning your torso to the right to shift into a horse stance. As you turn, pivot your left toes inward and angle your right toes slightly outward to enhance balance. Following the natural motion of your body, release your left hand from the cane and whip the cane with your right hand in an upper arc toward the west. Simultaneously, ward off with your left palm toward the east at shoulder height for protection. Keep both elbows slightly bent (Photo 23-1).

Movement 2:

Lower your hands in a smooth, outward-to-inward curved motion, crossing them in front of your abdomen. Your right hand holds the cane underneath, with the cane's tail pointing to the south (Photo 23-2).

Movement 3:

Turn your left toes slightly inward and shift your weight onto your left leg. Then, bring your right foot in toward your left, placing both feet about shoulder-width apart. At the same time, lift the cane in front of your chest with the tail pointing south. Let your elbows sink slightly and gently ward off to the sides, maintaining the right hand underneath the cane. Hold a centered and balanced stance (Photo 23-3).

Photo 23-3

Posture 24: Closing Form

Photo 24-1 Photo 24-2 Photo 24-3

Movement 1:

Extend your arms forward and separate your hands a bit wider than shoulder width with elbows sink slightly (Photo 24-1).

Movement 2:

Lower your hands to the sides of your hips with the cane's tail touching the floor just a bit side of your right small toe (Photo 24-2).

Movement 3:

Bring your left foot close to your right foot to finish the form (Photo 24-3)

金雞獨立

Golden Rooster Stands on One Leg

Part IV
Tai Chi Long Staff in Simplified Form 24

Posture 1: Opening Form

Photo 1-1　　　　　　　　　　Photo 1-2

Movement 1:

Commence by facing due south, with your feet standing side by side, supporting an upright torso. The long staff is positioned vertically, just a few inches to the side of your right toes, held lightly in your right hand. Direct your line of sight forward (Photo 1-1).

Note: The directional lines and vectors illustrated in Photo 1 delineate the movement trajectories depicted in the succeeding image, elaborated upon in the subsequent textual paragraph. This descriptive methodology persists throughout the remaining illustrations.

Movement 2:

Step your left foot sideways, bringing your feet to shoulder-width apart, with toes pointing relatively forward. Simultaneously, circle your left palm upward to the front of your upper chest in an outward curve, with the fingers pointing upward. The left palm begins from the left hip, extending out and upward, then arcs inward through the left shoulder area and draws in toward your centerline (Photo 1-2).

Posture 2: Part Wild Horse's Mane

Photo 2-1   Photo 2-2

Movement 1:

Sink your hips and bend your knees slightly, grounding yourself in a stable stance. Use the rebound energy generated by this downward motion to lift the staff upward with your right hand. At the same time, turn your torso to the left, allowing the staff—kept in a vertical position—to follow the rotation of your upper body. Simultaneously, catch the staff with your left hand, and hold it with both hands, bracing it toward your left front (east), as if warding off an incoming force from that direction (Photo 2-1).

Movement 2:

Slide your right hand downward to the tail end of the staff, while your left hand shifts to a position just below the midpoint. From there, rotate your torso to the northeast to lead the upper end of the staff in a counterclockwise arc, initiating a parrying motion that redirects an incoming force from the east toward the northeast corner. Continue this circular motion downward in a sweeping arc with your torso coiling back to your right, until the staff settles in front of your chest, with its tip pointing toward the southeast corner. Simultaneously, step your left foot outward to the left (east), holding most of your weight onto the right leg to form a partial horse stance (Photo 2-2).

Photo 2-3　　　　　　　Photo 2-4

Movement 3:

Shift your weight onto your left foot and bend your left knee to form a bow stance. With a coordinated motion, striking the left-hand end of the staff diagonally upward and outward across your front centerline, aiming toward your left front corner (northeast). At the same time, twist your right heel slightly backward to align with the leftward rotation of your torso. This striking motion toward the left rear corner is not driven by isolated arm movement, but by the integrated power of your entire body moving as a unified whole. You should feel the vibration of the staff rebounding back into your body, serving as feedback to test your structural alignment and firmness. Maintain your gaze on the left-hand end of the staff throughout the movement (Photo 2-3).

Movement 4:

Shift your weight back and lift your left toes, turning them outward to point toward the northeast. Then place your entire left foot firmly on the ground to reestablish a stable and rooted base. As you rotate your torso to the left, step your right foot in beside the left to close the stance in a centered position. At the same time, circle the left-hand end of the staff in a smooth clockwise arc above your head, as if redirecting or deflecting an incoming force away from your front. Simultaneously, switch the position of your hands—sliding the right hand upward and the left hand downward along the staff—to reset your grip for control and readiness. Let the movement be fluid, driven by the coordinated turning of your torso rather than isolated arm motion. As the motion concludes, position the staff diagonally and slightly vertical in front of your right chest, with the high end angled gently forward. Maintain a calm, focused demeanor with a unified structure, relaxed yet fully engaged (Photo 2-4).

Photo 2-5   Photo 2-6

Movement 5:

Turn your left toes slightly outward and rotate your torso to the southeast to lead the upper end of the staff in a clockwise arc, initiating a parrying motion that redirects an incoming force from the east toward the southeast corner. Continue this circular motion downward in a sweeping arc with your torso coiling back to your left, until the staff settles in front of your chest, with its tip pointing toward the northeast corner. Concurrently, advance the right foot laterally to the east, maintaining the majority of weight on the left leg to adopt a partial horse stance (Photo 2-5).

Movement 6:

Repeat Movement 3 and reversing "left" and "right" (Photo 2-6).

Photo 2-7

Photo 2-8   Photo 2-9

Movement 7:

Repeat Movement 4, 5, and 6 with reversing "left" and "right" (Photo 2-7, 2-8, 2-9).

Posture 3: White Crane Spreading Its Wings

Photo 3-1   Photo 3-2

Movement 1:

Step your right foot closer to your left foot while gently turning your torso to the left. Guide the upper end of the staff parrying in a small clockwise arc above your head, moving from the northeast corner to the southeast. At the same time, the lower end of the staff, held in your right hand, parries downward toward the front of your right knee. At the conclusion of the movement, hold the staff relatively vertical in front of your right chest, with your left hand positioned above the right. Your gaze should be directed toward the east (Photo 3-1).

Movement 2:

Turn your torso to the right and guide the right-hand end of the staff in a large clockwise arc, starting from your left front low quadrant (northeast), passing outside your left shoulder, and continuing to the right front high quadrant (southeast). Your left hand remains in contact with the staff throughout this motion, so that the staff ends up resting diagonally along the outside of your right arm. Simultaneously, step your left foot a half-step forward toward the east, placing the ball of the foot on the floor to create a slightly wider base of support, while keeping the majority of your weight centered on the right leg (Photo 3-2).

Photo 3-3

Movement 3:

Move your left foot slightly forward, and use your right hand to guide the high end of the staff upward and outward a bit farther, while your left hand parries in a curved path to the outside of your left hip. Maintain a softly rounded shape in both arms throughout the motion. Your body should remain relatively oriented toward the east (Photo 3-3).

Posture 4: Brush Knee on Both Sides

Photo 4-1   Photo 4-2

Movement 1:

Parry the high end of the staff in a counterclockwise downward arc, guided by a leftward twist of your torso. The torso leads your right hand to bring the staff from above the front of your head down toward the front of your left shoulder, as if deflecting an incoming strike to your face. Without pausing, rotate your torso back to the right—like releasing a coiled spring from the previous leftward motion—and allow this rebound to drive the right-hand end of the staff across your lower front and toward the outside of your right leg. As this happens, your left palm moves upward to assist in holding the staff vertically in front of your right side. At the same time, draw your left foot back closer to the right foot (Photo 4-1).

Movement 2:

Spin the vertical staff outside of your right shoulder, with your left hand positioned low and your right hand high. As the staff rotates, slide your left hand down to the end of the staff and anchor it against the left side of your ribs. Your right hand is just above your right shoulder, holding the staff in a diagonal position across your chest, with the right-hand end pointing toward the southeast high corner. At the same time, step your left foot out to the east (Photo 4-2).

Photo 4-3   Photo 4-4

Movement 3:

Turn your torso to the left and strike with the right-hand end of the staff, sweeping it from your right rear high corner (southwest) forward toward the east. Conclude the strike with the staff positioned a bit diagonally across your front, below chest level and above the knees. Due to the momentum generated by the full-body motion, it may be difficult to pinpoint an exact ending position—allow some flexibility and trust your internal sense of balance and control. Simultaneously, slide your right heel slightly backward to support and stabilize the forward strike. Be sure to engage the power of your entire body as one integrated unit—especially the rotation of your waist and torso, along with the internal flow of qi. Avoid relying on isolated arm strength alone. You should feel the vibration of the staff reverberate through your structure; this feedback is key to testing your alignment, connectivity, and rootedness (Photo 4-3).

Movement 4:

Shift your weight back and lift your left toes, turning them outward so they point toward the northeast. Then place your entire left foot firmly on the ground to reestablish a stable base. As you rotate your torso to the left, step your right foot in beside the left to close your stance. Simultaneously, circle the right-hand end of the staff in a counterclockwise arc above your head, as if redirecting or deflecting an incoming force away from your front. Let the motion flow smoothly, led by the coordinated turning of your torso. As the motion concludes, position the staff diagonally and slightly vertical in front of your left chest, with the high end angled gently forward, forming a protective guard. Maintain a relaxed yet ready posture, with your structure unified and your intention focused (Photo 4-4).

Photo 4-5　　　　　　Photo 4-6

Movement 5:

Without pausing, continue the motion by circling the upper end of the staff in a counterclockwise arc, moving from the front of your head toward your left rear high corner (northwest). As this arc unfolds, switch your hand positions—sliding your right hand down to the lower end of the staff and your left hand upward to grasp a bit below the middle section. This adjustment allows you to hold the staff diagonally across your chest, with your right hand positioned near the front of your right ribs and your left hand above and outside of your left shoulder. At the same time, step your right foot forward to the east, establishing a broader stance while keeping the majority of your weight grounded in your left leg, forming a stable partial horse stance (Photo 4-5).

Movement 6:

Repeat Movement 3 and reversing "left" and "right" (Photo 4-6).

Photo 4-7

Photo 4-8

Photo 4-9

Movement 7:

Repeat Movement 4, 5, and 6, and reversing "left" and "right" (Photo 4-7, 4-8, 4-9).

Posture 5: Playing a Guitar

Photo 5-1   Photo 5-2

Movement 1:

Step your right foot in closer to your left foot to generate forward momentum. Simultaneously, drive the staff forward with your left hand, as if thrusting a spear directly to the east. As the thrust extends, slide your right hand back until it meets your left hand, helping to extend the reach of the staff fully outward. At the completion of the motion, both hands should be positioned at the tail end of the staff, which is held horizontally at chest height. This posture is designed to train and test the strength of your arms and wrists with the internal qi that binds your body's connection with the staff. The weight of the staff can be a challenge to your wrists. Keep your knees bent and sink your hips down toward your heels to stabilize the forward strike with rooted strength and structure (Photo 5-1).

Movement 2:

At the end of the thrust, slide your right hand upward along the staff by about 8 to 10 inches to establish a pivot point. Then sharply jerk your left hand downward—from chest height to your lower abdomen. This action causes the far end of the staff to whip upward in a dynamic, upward-angled motion. Maintain your bent stance, keeping both hands lowered near knee level, while holding the staff diagonally and pointing to the east. The outer end of the staff should rise above head height, creating a powerful upward extension that reflects the force and control of the movement (Photo 5-2).

Photo 5-3

Movement 3:

Spin the outer end of the staff backward, guiding it toward the side of your right shoulder in a smooth, controlled motion. At the same time, slide your right hand upward along the staff to reposition your grip, while pushing the opposite end of the staff—starting from in front of your abdomen—outward toward the east. As this unfolds, move your left hand forward in front of your chest to grasp the staff just beyond its midpoint. Simultaneously, step your left foot forward in a half-step toward the east, while keeping the majority of your weight anchored on your right leg. At the conclusion of the movement, the staff should be held diagonally across your body: the left-hand end positioned forward at approximately head height, and the right hand near your right chest, with the tail of the staff extending behind your right waist. This closing posture represents the traditional "Hold the Guitar" pose, symbolizing both readiness and harmony, with the body and staff unified in balance and control (Photo 5-3).

Posture 6: Repulse Monkey

Photo 6-1   Photo 6-2

Movement 1:

Twist your right heel slightly backward to open the space between your legs, and step your left foot back toward the west. Keep the majority of your weight anchored on your right leg in front. At the same time, pull your right hand back to just above your right shoulder, while sliding your left hand to the tail end of the staff. Hold the staff above your right shoulder in a diagonal position, with the left-hand end slightly lower in front of your chest and the right-hand end extending westward at head height (Photo 6-1).

Movement 2:

Shift your weight back onto your left leg and rotate your torso to the left. As your body turns, strike the tail end of the staff in an upward and forward arc toward the east. At the end of the motion, the staff is relatively horizontal, pointing and guarding toward the eastern direction. Sink your hips and lower your stance into a stable partial horse stance, with the majority of your weight rooted through your left leg (Photo 6-2).

Photo 6-3   Photo 6-4

Movement 3:

Parry the outer end of the staff backward along the outside of your right leg in a smooth, controlled motion. At the same time, pull your right leg back and bring your right foot close to your left ankle. You may either rest your right toes lightly on the floor or, if your balance and leg strength allow, keep the right foot slightly lifted in the air. Hold the staff in a near-vertical position just outside your right leg, with the right-hand end lowered and the left-hand end raised above your head, as if setting up a protective guard along your right side. Make sure you leave enough length of the staff (about 2 feet) above your left hand (Photo 6-3).

Movement 4:

Twist your left heel slightly outward to widen the space between your legs, creating room for your right foot to retreat smoothly. Then step your right foot backward toward the west, keeping the majority of your weight anchored on your left leg to maintain a stable foundation. Simultaneously, spin the right-hand end of the staff backward and lift the staff slightly above your head, moving it from the side of your right shoulder across the top of your head toward the left. As the staff transitions, release your right hand and regrasp it in front of your left hand, adjusting your grip to maintain a good control. At the end of the motion, the staff rests diagonally above your left shoulder, with the left-hand end elevated and pointing west, and the right-hand end lowered in front of your left chest (Photo 6-4).

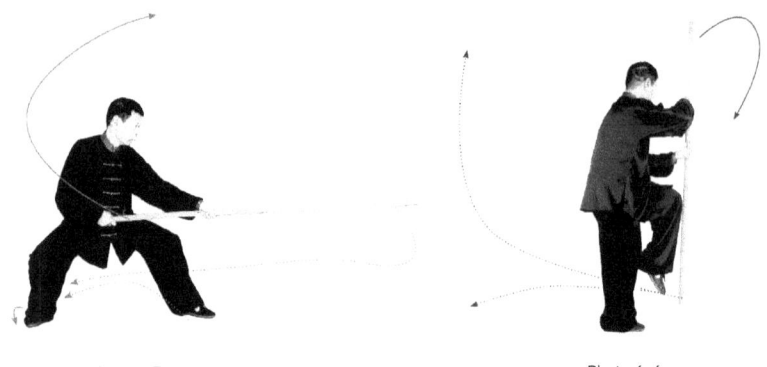

Photo 6-5   Photo 6-6

Movement 5:

Repeat Movement 2, and reversing "left" and "right" (Photo 6-5).

Movement 6:

Repeat Movement 3, and reversing "left" and "right" (Photo 6-6).

Photo 6-7   Photo 6-8

Movement 7:

Repeat Movement 4, and reversing "left" and "right" (Photo 6-7).

Movement 8:

Repeat Movement 2 (Photo 6-8).

Photo 6-9

Photo 6-10

Photo 6-11

Movement 9:

Repeat Movement 3, 4, 5 (Photo 6-9, 6-10, 6-11).

Posture 7: Grasp the Bird's Tail - Left

Photo 7-1   Photo 7-2

Movement 1:

Shift your weight slightly forward onto your left leg to establish a stable base for the upcoming movement. Simultaneously, lift the left-hand end of the staff while pressing down the right-hand end, initiating a controlled clockwise twist to parry the staff through a smooth half-circle arc in front of you, transforming it from a forward-pointing horizontal position into a vertical alignment. The movement mimics deflecting an incoming thrust directly toward your head, positioning the staff upright in front of your torso in a protective guard (Photo 7-1).

Movement 2:

Shift your weight onto your left leg, settling into a stable bow stance. As you do so, fold your left arm inward to transition the staff from a vertical to a horizontal position, with your left hand on top and your right hand supporting from below. The staff now rests horizontally in front of your upper chest, aligned parallel to your shoulders. Your forearms, softly rounded and enclosing the staff between them, create a solid and expansive frame—like a protective shield—establishing a strong ward-off posture that embodies both inner stability and outward readiness (Photo 7-2).

Photo 7-3   Photo 7-4

Movement 3:

Unfold your left arm and initiate a broad counterclockwise circular motion with both arms, guiding the left-hand end of the staff to draw a wide arc—from the outside of your right shoulder (south), sweeping across the high front of your head, and extending toward your left side (north). As the arc completes, rotate your torso to the right and shift your weight onto your right leg, allowing the momentum to carry the staff's outer end in a sweeping motion from the low northeast quadrant up to the high southwest quadrant. Coordinate this sweeping action by turning your right toes outward to support the rotation of your torso and deepen the movement. At the end of the motion, your hands hold the staff in a slightly vertical alignment—left hand positioned in front of your right shoulder, right hand reaching behind your right hip—with the upper end of the staff pointing diagonally upward above your head. Like waving a large flag, this sweeping motion embodies the essence of a Tai Chi roll-back—expansive, rooted, and fluid. It captures the idea of yielding with structure and redirecting force with grace. As the staff arcs across space, your body and intention move as one, expressing the dynamic softness and spiraling strength that define the roll-back posture in Tai Chi (Photo 7-3).

Movement 4:

Turn your torso back to the left and slide your right hand upward, positioning it just a few inches below your left hand on the staff. Follow the momentum of your leftward rotation to face east as you shift your weight onto your left leg, forming a left bow stance. At the same time, press the vertical staff firmly toward the east, expressing a clear forward intention. To support this press energy, adjust your right foot by twisting the heel slightly backward, anchoring your structure and aligning with the direction of force. This movement embodies the "press" energy in Tai Chi—rooted, directed, and unified through whole-body coordination (Photo 7-4).

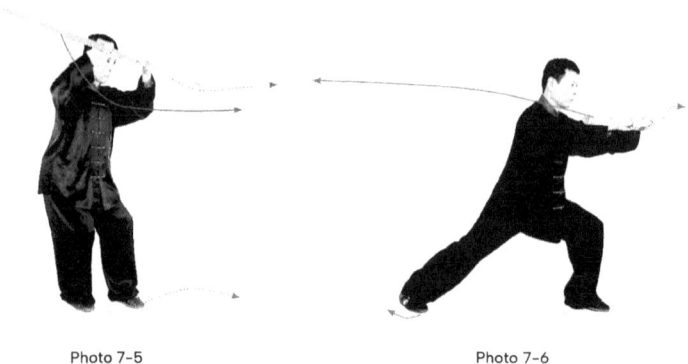

Photo 7-5   Photo 7-6

Movement 5:

Begin by spinning the staff in a smooth clockwise arc, transitioning it from a vertical to a horizontal position in front of your chest. As the staff turns, release and regrasp with your right hand, adjusting your grip for stability and control. At the same time, shift your weight back onto your right leg, and draw your left foot inward, placing it gently in front of your right foot for a compact stance. Simultaneously, draw both hands back, guiding the staff upward in a gentle curve until it forms a horizontal shield in front of your forehead. This motion simulates an upward parry, establishing a moment of guarded readiness with the staff parallel to the ground (Photo 7-5).

Movement 6:

With a brief moment of pause, step your left foot outward toward the east, and shift your weight forward into a grounded left bow stance. At the same time, lower the staff from your forehead to chest level, then strike it forward with both hands, extending your arms naturally with relaxed yet engaged elbows. Keep your eyes focused straight ahead, projecting intent and awareness toward the direction of the push. This movement embodies the Tai Chi principle of unified force, where the energy of the entire body channels pushing through the staff. Use the feedback of the push to test your structural alignment, rooted stance, and internal cohesion (Photo 7-6).

Posture 8: Grasp the Bird's Tail - Right

Photo 8-1 Photo 8-2

Movement 1:

Turn your right toes slightly outward to protect your knee joints and maintain healthy structural alignment. As you shift your weight onto your right leg, begin to rotate your torso to the right, initiating the movement from your waist. Simultaneously, strike the right-hand end of the staff toward the west in a gentle upward arc. Keep your arms softly rounded, maintaining the integrity of a ward-off shape. This posture embodies both defense and readiness. Focus on the fluid coordination between your torso rotation and staff rightward strike, allowing your power to be expressed from the ground up through the waist and shoulders—not just the arms alone (Photo 8-1).

Movement 2:

Turn the toes of your left foot slightly inward as you rotate your torso gently to the right, initiating a subtle spiral through your body. As your torso turns, move your right hand in a downward and inward arc to bring it in front of your chest, at the same time, pivot on your right thumb to rotate your other four fingers from above the staff to underneath, smoothly adjusting your grip. Hold the staff horizontally above your right forearm with your left palm touching on the staff supporting your right palm's move. Simultaneously, shift your weight fully onto your left leg and lift your right knee to abdomen height, rising into a balanced left-legged rooster stance. Keep your spine upright, arms softly rounded, and eyes looking to the right, maintaining internal focus and structural integrity (Photo 8-2).

Photo 8-3

Movement 3:

Turn your torso to the right and raise your right hand to lift the staff horizontally above your head. Using the spiraling energy of your torso, twirl the staff in a full, smooth circle with your right hand, allowing the motion to express both control and fluidity. As the circle completes, lower your right hand and fold your right arm inward and downward in front of your chest. Simultaneously, bend your left arm inward to support the staff from beneath. The staff now rests horizontally across your upper chest, parallel to your shoulders. Your forearms, gently rounded and enclosing the staff, form a firm and expansive warding-off frame. Following the momentum of the rightward turn, step your right foot westward and shift your weight into a right bow stance. To support the direction of the ward-off, twist your left heel slightly backward, anchoring your structure as your arms and the staff project strength and protection toward the west (Photo 8-3).

Photo 8-4　　　　　　　　　　Photo 8-5

Movement 4:

Repeat the Movement 3 in Posture 7: Grasp the Bird's Tail - Left, and reversing "left" and "right" (Photo 8-4).

Movement 5:

Repeat the Movement 4 in Posture 7: Grasp the Bird's Tail - Left, and reversing "left" and "right" (Photo 8-5). Optionally, you can move your left hand above the right hand to hold the staff in a vertical position before pressing it toward the west. This variation may offer a more controlled structure for some practitioners. If you are right-handed, you might find that keeping your right hand underneath provides better control and stability when directing the staff. Choose the hand placement that best aligns with your natural strength and coordination, while maintaining integrity in structure and intent.

Photo 8-6   Photo 8-7

Movement 6:

Repeat the Movement 5, and 6 in Posture 7: Grasp the Bird's Tail - Left, and reversing "left" and "right" (Photo 8-6, 8-7).

Posture 9: Single Whip

Photo 9-1   Photo 9-2

Movement 1:

Sink your right hip and shift your weight toward your left foot, creating a grounded and rooted base. As you do so, turn your left toes slightly outward to protect your left knee from strain and improve alignment. Simultaneously, rotate your torso to the left, move the left-hand end of the staff in a smooth parrying arc toward the outside of your left shoulder. Be mindful that the staff and your body move as a unified whole, connected through your center and driven by internal energy (Photo 9-1).

Movement 2:

Continue turning your torso further to the left, deepening the spiral and engaging the waist and spine. At the same time, spin the left-hand end of the staff downward in a controlled arc to guard the outside of your left hip. This sets up a dynamic strike with the right-hand end of the staff, which whips forward toward the southeast at head height, as if intercepting an incoming force. Direct your gaze toward the southeast, following the line of energy and intent. Let the power of the movement originate from the coiling of your torso, not just the arms, to maintain internal connection and fluidity (Photo 9-2).

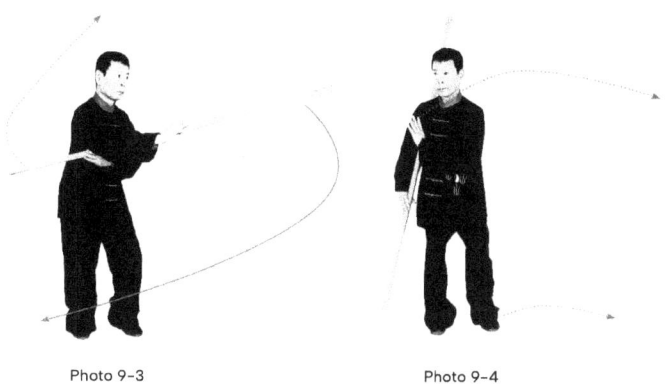

Photo 9-3   Photo 9-4

Movement 3:

Turn your torso to the right and sweep the right-hand end of the staff downward, paddling it across the outside of your right leg. Simultaneously, arc the left-hand end of the staff upward from the outside of your left hip to the front of your chest, mimicking the motion of kayaking through water. Without pausing, continue the circular momentum by raising the right-hand end of the staff from behind your right shoulder, while pressing the left-hand end downward past the outside of your right hip. Allow the motion to flow continuously in a smooth orbit, completing a full circle with the right-hand end returning to its original position. By the end of the movement, the left-hand end of the staff has transitioned from the outside of your left hip to behind your right shoulder, with your left hand now tucked under your right armpit. At the same time, draw your left foot inward, placing it lightly next to your right foot with the toes gently touching the floor for balance and readiness (Photo 9-3).

Movement 4:

Release your left hand from the staff and continue paddling the right-hand end downward in a smooth, arcing motion. Let your right hand drop naturally to the side of your right hip as the staff rotates into a vertical position behind your right shoulder. At this point, the upper end of the staff rises behind and above your head, while the lower end aligns just outside your right ankle, so the staff neatly aligns alongside your right leg. Simultaneously, raise your left palm in front of your right chest in a guarding gesture, ready to engage or redirect incoming force (Photo 9-4).

Photo 9-5

Movement 5:

Turn your torso to the left and step your left foot forward toward the east, settling into a strong, grounded left bow stance. Simultaneously, whip your left palm in a smooth, striking arc from the front of your right chest across your face toward the left at shoulder height. In coordination with this motion, execute a controlled parry by drawing the right-hand end of the staff backward, creating a balanced counterforce that maintains the structure and integrity of the movement. At the end of the motion, the staff aligns diagonally at the back across your body, matching the diagonal stretch formed by your extended right leg and the forward-leaning alignment of your torso (Photo 9-5).

Posture 10: Wave Hands Like Clouds

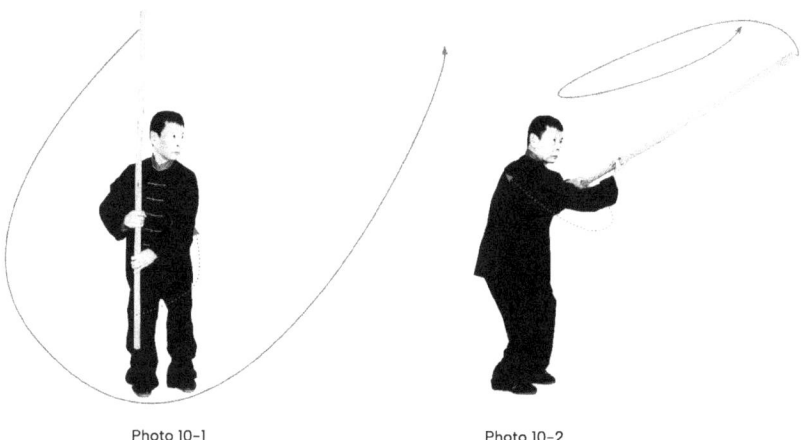

Photo 10-1   Photo 10-2

Movement 1:

Begin by turning your torso slightly to the left while using your right hand to sling the upper end of the staff in a broad clockwise arc, starting high from behind your right shoulder. Sweep it low outside and in front of your right leg, then bring it back up in a rising arc to above the front of your right shoulder, completing a full circle. As the arc finishes, catch the staff with your left hand approximately eight inches below your right hand. At the same time, draw your right foot in closer to your left, establishing a compact and centered stance. Hold the staff relatively vertical in front of your right chest with both palms facing inward. This circling movement of the staff acts as a clearing or deflecting action, creating a protective shield along the right side of your body (Photo 10-1).

Movement 2:

Without pausing, continue the momentum by twisting your torso to the left while maintaining the clockwise rotation of the staff. This motion drives an upward, slicing strike toward your right front high corner (southeast), similar to an uppercut. At the end of the movement, the left-hand end of the staff settles near the front of your left chest, while the outer end extends high above your head. Direct your gaze toward the raised tip of the staff, maintaining alignment and focus (Photo 10-2).

Photo 10-3   Photo 10-4

Movement 3:

Maintaining your compact and centered stance, twist your torso deeply to the left to build internal torque, then immediately reverse the motion, coiling back to the right. This sharp rebound leads the outer end of the staff in a powerful U-turn arc, swinging it high above your head from the southeast, sweeping toward your back left corner (northwest), and circling forward again to the northeast upper corner. At the end of the movement, your forearms cross—your right hand positioned on top, and your left forearm tucked beneath—holding the staff diagonally with the left-hand end near the outside of your right shoulder (southwest). The outer tip of the staff points forward to the northeast at head height. This flowing, spiraled action should be powered by your torso's coiling and uncoiling energy, ensuring the staff's momentum comes from the whole-body integration for effective parrying and deflection (Photo 10-3).

Movement 4:

Twist your left heel outward toward the northeast to initiate and support a rightward spiral of your torso toward the southwest corner. Use this coiling momentum to lead the outer end of the staff in a sweeping arc above your head, striking downward toward the outside of your right shoulder. Your arms should now be roughly parallel, holding the staff diagonally in front of your forehead, with the outer end tilted downward to shoulder height. This posture forms a strong, shield-like structure while channeling the spiral energy from the ground through your core into the staff (Photo 10-4).

Photo 10-5 Photo 10-6

Movement 5:

Paddle the right-hand end of the staff downward in a smooth arc from the high southwest quadrant to the outside of your right foot. Simultaneously, rotate the left-hand end of the staff upward in front of your face, creating a dynamic spiraling motion. By the end of the movement, the staff stands vertically along your right front quadrant with your left hand on top of the right hand, effectively forming a fencing structure that guards the right side of your body toward the southwest. Allow the twisting of your torso and arms to drive the staff with internal cohesion and precision (Photo 10-5).

Movement 6:

Without pausing, initiate a vertical spinning circle of the staff behind your right rear corner, moving diagonally from the southwest through to the northeast. Begin the motion by pushing the left-hand end of the staff toward the southwest, then immediately release your left hand to allow the momentum to flow freely. Let your torso's coiling motion and your right arm's control guide the staff through the complete arc. As the circle completes, regrasp the staff with your left hand beneath your right, which is now on top with the palm facing outward. The staff once again stands vertically along your right front quadrant, but with the grip reversed—ready for the next movement (Photo 10-6).

Photo 10-7

Movement 7:

Push your left hand to put the left-hand side of the staff beneath your right armpit, guiding it to the outside of your right ribs. Simultaneously, spin the right-hand end of the staff in a downward arc from high to low along the outside of your right leg, effectively inverting the staff and tucking it behind your right arm in a concealed, compact position. As this action unfolds, step your left foot toward the east, establishing a stable base. Keep your left palm in a parrying gesture at the front of your right chest maintaining a guarded, coiled posture (Photo 10-7).

Photo 10-8   Photo 10-9

Part IV: Tai Chi Long Staff in Simplified Form 24

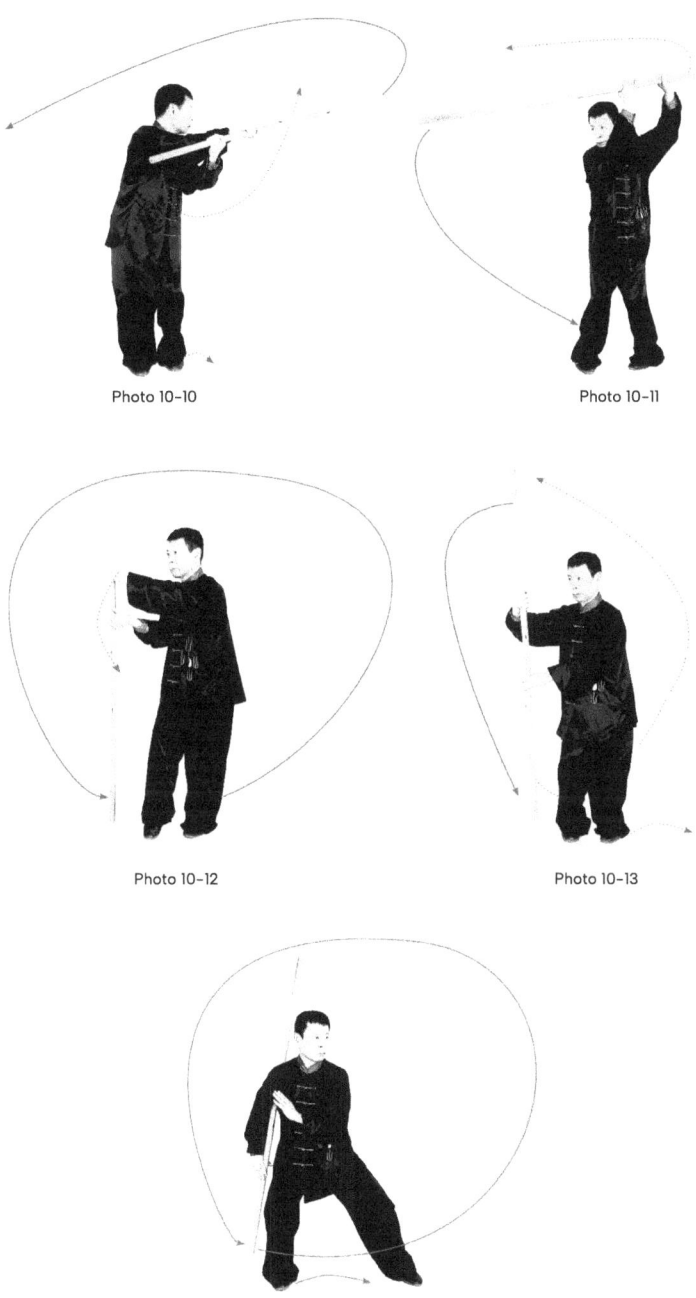

Photo 10-10

Photo 10-11

Photo 10-12

Photo 10-13

Photo 10-14

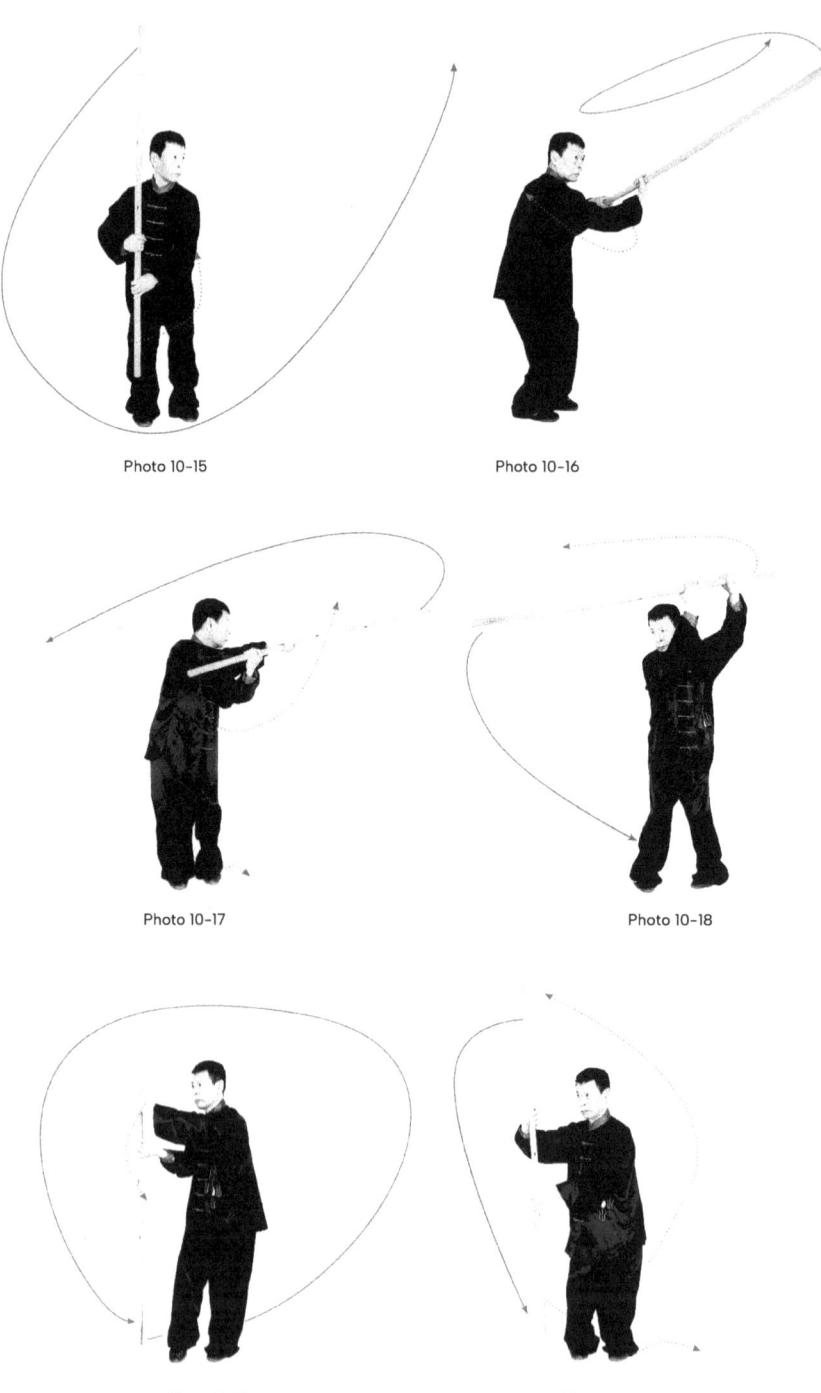

Photo 10-15

Photo 10-16

Photo 10-17

Photo 10-18

Photo 10-19

Photo 10-20

Movement 8:

Repeat Movements 1 through 7 in two continuous cycles to complete the "Wave Hands Like Clouds" sequence. As you flow through these motions, allow the staff to circle smoothly around your body, guiding its energy with your torso's rotation and coordinated footwork. With each cycle, step gradually toward the east, advancing with three steady steps. Maintain a calm and rooted demeanor as the staff traces elegant arcs through space, embodying both defense and fluid power. This sequence culminates in a harmonious blend of movement and intention, with the staff seamlessly weaving around your form in rhythmic waves (Photo 10-8 through 10-21).

Photo 10-21

Posture 11: Single Whip

Photo 11-1

Movement 1:

Turn your torso to the left and step your left foot forward toward the east, settling into a strong and balanced left bow stance. Simultaneously, whip your left palm from the front of your right chest across your face to the east at shoulder height. In harmony with this motion, draw the right-hand end of the staff backward in a controlled parry and twist your right heel a bit back, creating a dynamic yet stable counterforce that reinforces the structural integrity of your posture. At the conclusion of the movement, the staff lies diagonally across the back of your body, mirroring the extended line formed by your right leg and the forward-leaning alignment of your torso, embodying both rooted strength and expansive energy (Photo 11-1).

Posture 12: High Pat on Horse

Photo 12-1   Photo 12-2

Movement 1:

Step your right foot forward by half a step, bringing it closer to your left foot, and shift your weight onto your right leg to form a left empty stance. At the same time, parry the right-hand end of the staff forward to the front of your right foot, holding it relatively vertical between your right arm and the right side of your ribs to create a subtle guard. As you make this transition, draw your left palm slightly back in front of your chest, maintaining a softly rounded protective posture facing east. Keep your arms relaxed yet engaged, ready to respond with fluidity and intention (Photo 12-1).

Movement 2:

Without pausing, extend the right-hand end of the staff forward in a striking poke, with the staff held horizontally beneath your right arm. Align your right arm with the direction of the staff, pointing toward the east with unified intention. Simultaneously, sweep your left hand downward in a smooth arc toward the front of your left hip, complementing the staff strike with balance and fluidity. Lightly lift your left heel to allow your torso to straighten and expand upward, completing the motion with poised energy and integrated structure (Photo 12-2).

Posture 13: Kick with Right Heel

Photo 13-1　　　　　　　　　　Photo 13-2

Movement 1:

Parry the right-hand end of the staff toward the northeast corner as your right forearm rounds inward across the front of your chest. At the same time, raise your left palm from the side of your left hip to cross gently above your right wrist, forming a soft arc. Keep both arms rounded to shape a shield-like, protective frame in front of your upper body. Simultaneously, step your left foot toward the northeast, preparing your stance for the next movement (Photo 13-1).

Movement 2:

As you settle into a rooted left-sided bow stance, extend your left palm in a parrying motion toward the left front (northeast), rising just above your forehead to create a high protective arc. At the same time, sweep the right-hand end of the staff diagonally downward toward the right front (southwest), guiding it to hip height. At the end of the movement, your right forearm tucks the staff securely under your right armpit and along your back, forming a compact and controlled hold. This coordinated action mimics the redirection of an incoming force, combining dynamic spiral energy with stable structure. Keep both arms softly rounded to maintain the integrity of the warding-off shape and full spatial awareness (Photo 13-2).

Photo 13-3 Photo 13-4

Movement 3:

Parry the right-hand end of the staff in a downward-then-upward curve and bring your right hand back in front of your chest, and move downward and inward your left palm until it cross on top of the right wrist again in front of your chest, with your right hand holding the staff diagonally underneath. Simultaneously, lift your right knee up to abdomen height, balancing on your left leg in a stable left-leg rooster stance, with your right toes pointing diagonally downward. Engage your core to maintain balance and stability in this poised position (Photo 13-3).

Movement 4:

Open both arms to the sides at shoulder height, and parry the right-hand end of the staff upward toward the southeast upper quadrant, keeping both elbows softly bent to preserve structure and flow. Simultaneously, execute a right front kick toward the southeast corner, leading with the heel and keeping your gaze focused on the kicking foot. The staff should remain securely tucked under your right arm, aligned along your right rib cage for control and stability. Your right arm stays parallel to your extended leg, forming a unified line of force. Maintain centered balance and full-body coordination throughout this dynamic action to ensure precision and rooted strength (Photo 13-4).

Posture 14: Strike Opponent's Ears with Both Fists

Photo 14-1   Photo 14-2

Movement 1:

Draw your right leg back, then place it down toward the southeast corner in a controlled and mindful landing. As your foot descends, parry the right-hand end of the staff in a smooth inward arc from head height downward, clearing the southeast space and finishing in front of your right knee. At the same time, guide your left hand inward to the front of your chest, then sweep it down to waist height in a soft parrying motion with the palm facing up. Maintain your weight primarily on your left leg, holding a stable right-foot empty stance. Stay focused on your right front corner, with your upper body poised and alert (Photo 14-1).

Movement 2:

Parry the right-hand end of the staff from the front of your right foot, circling it behind your right leg toward the northwest corner, then sling it upward in a spiraling strike toward the high southeast quadrant. Simultaneously, shift your weight forward onto your right leg, forming a strong and rooted right bow stance. Bring your left hand under your right armpit to hold and assist in stabilizing the staff. Maintain structural integrity with relaxed shoulders, slightly lowered elbows, and softly rounded arms, allowing for controlled power and fluid movement. This movement is aiming the opponent's left ear (Photo 14-2).

Part IV: Tai Chi Long Staff in Simplified Form 24

Photo 14-3

Movement 3:

Maintaining a stable stance, rotate your torso to the left and spiral your left hand outward from beneath your right armpit, initiating a sweeping arc with the left-hand end of the staff. Guide it from your right rear corner, across the front of your right leg, and down toward your left rear low quadrant (northwest) in a smooth, spiraling motion. Without pausing, twist your torso sharply back to the right, using the coiled energy of your waist to strike the left-hand end of the staff upward in a dynamic arc—from the low northwest to the high southeast quadrant, aiming at the opponent's right ear. This coordinated movement draws a reversed S-shaped path for the left-hand end of the staff: first from the low "tail" to the high "head" of the S, and finally extending out toward the southeast. Simultaneously, the right-hand end of the staff carves a flatter S shape from the front of your body toward your right rear quadrant, pointing northwest. The spiraling torque of your torso drives this intricate dual-path motion. Conclude with the staff held horizontally at head height, both hands gripping firmly to project control, energy, and readiness (Photo 14-3).

Posture 15: Kick with Left Heel

Photo 15-1   Photo 15-2

Movement 1:

Sink your hips and draw your left heel inward while turning your right toes slightly inward to align both knees comfortably and protect your joints. Simultaneously, rotate your torso to the left and spin the staff approximately 180 degrees to strike with the left-hand end toward the northwest corner. Maintain a rounded arm structure, with both elbows gently sunk to preserve a stable, ward-off energy and balanced posture (Photo 15-1).

Movement 2:

Continue rotating your torso slightly to the left and, at the same time, push the staff horizontally across the top of your head—from in front of your face to the left shoulder side. Release your right hand from the staff and position your right palm in front of your chest in a guarding gesture. Let the staff rest momentarily across your left arm and shoulder, forming a shield-like structure. Meanwhile, shift your weight onto your right leg and draw your left foot inward, placing the toes lightly on the floor beside your right foot to establish a poised and balanced stance (Photo 15-2).

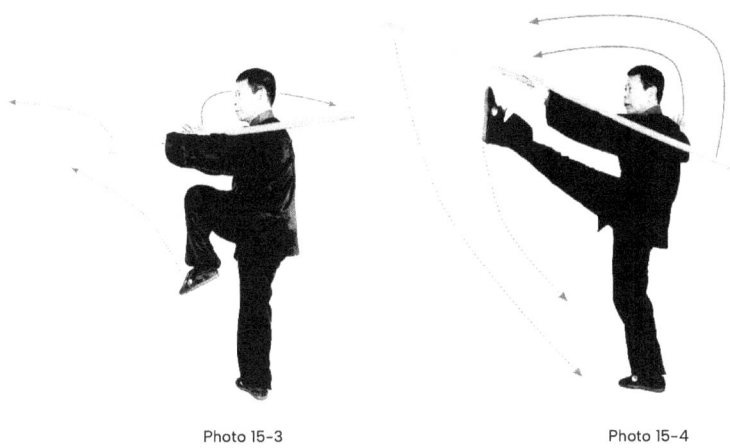

Photo 15-3　　　　　　　　　　　Photo 15-4

Movement 3:

Lift your left foot, raising the knee to abdomen height. Maintain a steady rooster stance, balancing on your right foot, and direct your gaze toward the northwest corner (Photo 15-3).

Movement4:

Parry the left-hand end of the staff upward toward the northwest upper quadrant while extending your right arm to the east at shoulder height. Simultaneously, execute a left front kick toward the northwest corner, leading with the heel and keeping your eyes focused on the kicking foot. The staff should remain firmly held in your left hand, aligned along your left arm, and positioned above the kicking left leg. Maintain centered balance and coordinated whole-body movement to ensure precision, control, and rooted strength throughout this dynamic action (Photo 15-4).

Posture 16: Golden Rooster Stands on One Leg - Left

Photo 16-1   Photo 16-2

Movement 1:

Draw your left foot inward close to your right leg and keep it lifted, if your balance allows, or let the left foot toes lightly touch the floor for your balance . At the same time, turn your torso to face the west and parry the left-hand end of the staff downward to the outside of your left leg. Grasp the upper end of the staff with your right hand in front of your head, while adjusting your left hand to grip the middle section of the staff with the palm facing outward. The staff is held vertically in front of your body, forming a warding-off structure toward the west (Photo 16-1).

Movement 2:

Step your left foot out toward the west at a slight angle to the southwest, settling into a partial horse stance with your weight primarily on your right leg. At the same time, rotate the vertical staff by guiding the left-hand end toward your rear left corner (southeast), then circle it upward past the outside of your left shoulder, finishing with a dynamic strike to the west at knee height. At the end of the motion, the staff should be held horizontally, parallel to the floor—your left hand positioned in front of your left knee, and your right hand aligned in front of your lower right abdomen. This movement also serves as a form of strength and structure training. You should feel the feedback of the staff's vibration pulsing back through your arms. Be sure to grip the staff firmly and stay rooted, allowing that vibrational force to test your structural alignment and the integrated wholeness of your body (Photo 16-2).

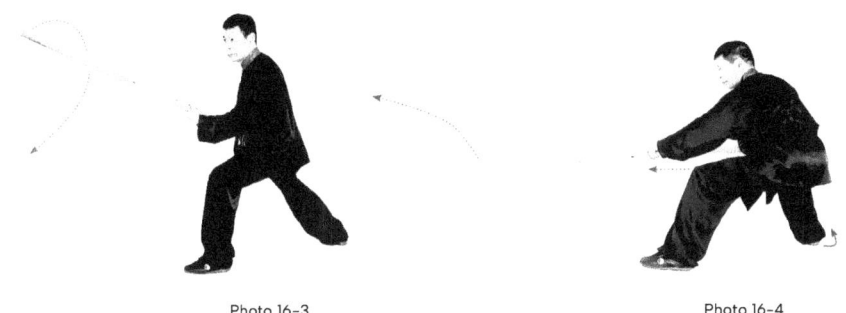

Photo 16-3   Photo 16-4

Movement 3:

Deflect the outer end of the staff outward in a counterclockwise half-circle spiral toward the southwest. As you do this, shift your weight onto your left leg, forming a rooted left bow stance to drive the outer end of the staff slightly forward. Power the movement with your legs and waist, using coordinated hip and shoulder rotation to guide the staff in a smooth, curved path. Your right hand anchors the rear end of the staff to your right abdomen, connecting to your dantian and initiating the motion with silk-reeling energy. This redirection technique, adapted from traditional spearmanship, allows you to neutralize incoming force without confronting it directly (Photo 16-3).

Movement4:

Sink your hips and waist, optionally shifting some weight back toward your right leg to generate a dynamic rebound. Then spiral the outer end of the staff inward and downward in a clockwise half-circle, simulating the action of wrapping and suppressing an opponent's weapon toward your center. This technique, also derived from spearmanship, is a control method used to off-balance and destabilize the opponent. The movement is powered by the torque of your torso, serving as a natural counter to the previous deflection, and enhances both control and flow in your technique (Photo 16-4).

Photo 16-5   Photo 16-6

Movement 5:

Compress your body momentarily, then explode forward by driving from the rear leg, launching the outer end of the staff in a powerful, level thrust toward the west. As you thrust, slide your left hand back to meet your right hand near the base, ensuring firm control. Snap both wrists subtly to accelerate the tip of the staff while maintaining full-body coordination and alignment. You may twist your right heel backward to reinforce the forward drive and unify the action. The thrust must be fast, direct, and penetrating—like a snake striking—focused and unhesitating. Your body, arms, and staff should form a single, cohesive line of energy. This represents the signature finishing move in traditional spearplay, applied here in staff technique to deliver a decisive end to the encounter (Photo 16-5).

Movement 6:

Lift the outer end of the staff in a rising arc to spin it up and over your head, using the downward press of the handle end in front of your left knee as the pivot point. At the same time, slide your left hand upward along the shaft, release your right hand, and then re-grasp the upper section of the staff with your right hand in front of your right shoulder with the palm facing out toward the northwest. As this coordinated transition occurs, step your right foot in beside your left foot, creating a compact and rooted stance. This motion rotates the staff from a horizontal strike position to a vertical guard, aligning the staff upright in front of your body. The final posture presents a solid vertical guard facing west, combining agility, control, and readiness (Photo 16-6).

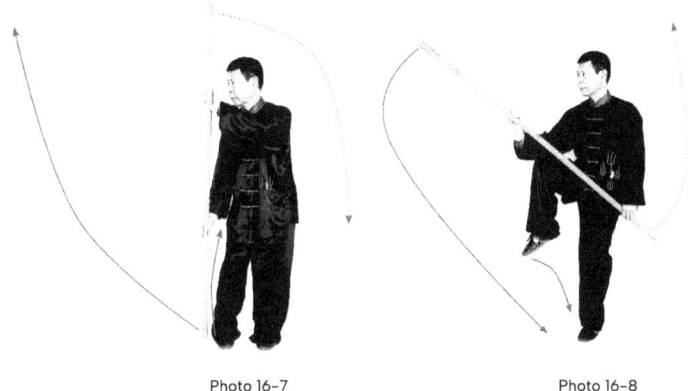

Photo 16-7   Photo 16-8

Movement 7:

Rotate your torso slightly to the left and initiate a spiraling motion of the staff by driving the right-hand end downward past the outside of your right shoulder, continuing down to the front of your right foot. Simultaneously, the left-hand end arcs upward to position in front of your right shoulder, with your left palm facing outward toward the southwest. The spin is powered primarily by your torso rotation, not arm strength—allow your arms to follow the momentum generated by your core (Photo 16-7).

Movement 8:

Without pausing, continue the spin by pulling the left-hand end downward and backward to the outside of your left hip, using this recoil to launch the right-hand end upward in a striking arc toward the west. At the same time, raise your right knee to waist level, with the toes angled downward in a left rooster stance. At the end of this movement, the staff is held diagonally across your body, both hands firmly gripping it—aligned toward the west, expressing balance, control, and readiness (Photo 16-8).

Posture 17: Golden Rooster Stands on One Leg - Right

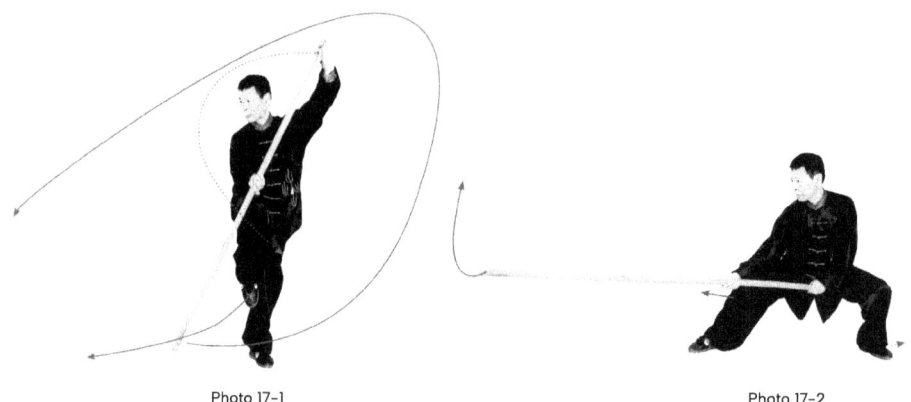

Photo 17-1   Photo 17-2

Movement 1:

Parry the higher end of the staff in a leftward and downward arc toward the southwest low quadrant, using a controlled, circular motion. As you do this, slide your left hand up to take hold of the higher end of the staff, while simultaneously adjusting your right hand's grip—rotating the thumb to the opposite side to prepare for the next maneuver. At the end of this coordinated movement, the right-hand end of the staff is angled diagonally across your body in front of your right leg, while your right knee remains lifted in a poised left-legged rooster stance, maintaining balance and readiness (Photo 17-1).

Movement 2:

Repeat Movement 2 of Posture 16: Left Lower Form and Stand on One Leg, reversing the facing direction as well as the left and right hand and foot (Photo 17-2).

Photo 17-3   Photo 17-4

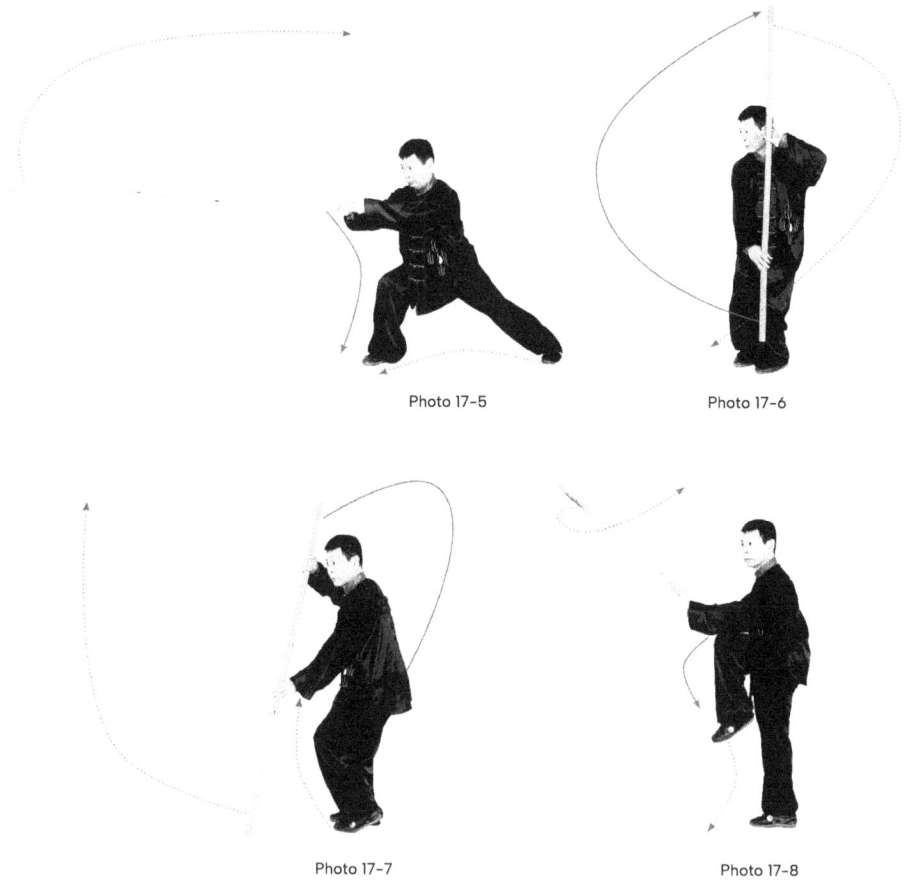

Photo 17-5   Photo 17-6

Photo 17-7   Photo 17-8

Movement 3:

Repeat Movements 3 through 8 of Posture 16: Left Lower Form and Stand on One Leg, reversing the facing direction as well as the left and right hand and foot (Photo 17-3 through 17-8).

Posture 18: Fair Lady Works with Shuttles on Both Sides

Photo 18-1   Photo 18-2

Movement 1:

Step down your left foot, angling the toes outward toward the southwest corner. As you do this, push the right-hand end of the staff downward while turning your torso to face the southwest. Hold the staff vertically in front of your left leg in a protective parry. At the same time, shift your weight onto your left foot, allowing the right heel to lift with the toes lightly touching the ground, establishing a responsive, rooted stance (Photo 18-1).

Movement 2:

Step your right foot toward the northwest corner, and twist the right-hand end of the staff in a clockwise arc from the southwest low quadrant up to the northwest high quadrant. As the motion completes, hold the staff diagonally across your chest—your right hand extended toward the northwest at shoulder height, and left hand lower, positioned near the front of your left ribs. Ensure the rotation is driven by your waist and torso, allowing the arms to follow naturally and preserving full-body integration (Photo 18-2).

Part IV: Tai Chi Long Staff in Simplified Form 24

Photo 18-3

Movement 3:

Without pausing, rotate your torso fully to face the northwest and shift weight to the right leg into a right bow stance, and swing the left-hand end of the staff in a powerful clockwise arc—starting from behind your left hip, sweeping upward and forward to the front of your head (northwest). As you strike, twist your left heel backward to reinforce the movement with whole-body torque and stability. At the end of the motion, the staff is held diagonally in front of your head—your left arm extended high and outward, while your right arm is rounded, positioning the right-hand end of the staff behind your right shoulder, pointing to the southeast. Keep your eyes focused on the left-hand end of the staff, maintaining alignment, intention, and spatial awareness (Photo 18-3).

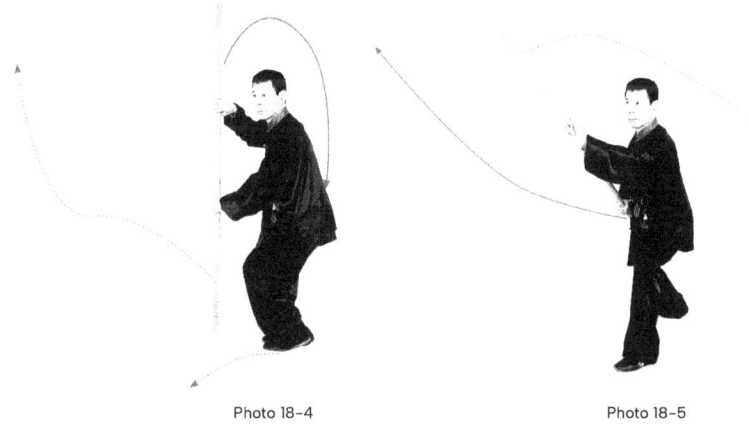

Photo 18-4   Photo 18-5

Movement 4:

Turn your torso to the left (toward the southwest) and guide the left-hand end of the staff downward in a parrying motion to the lower front of your legs, while simultaneously pushing the right-hand end of the staff upward in front of your head. This action brings the staff into a vertical guarding position aligned with the southwest direction. At the same time, draw your left foot in beside your right foot, forming a compact, stable base positioned safely behind the protective line of the staff. Keep your gaze focused toward the southwest corner, maintaining a ready awareness and centered balance (Photo 18-4).

Movement 5:

Repeat Movements 2, reversing the facing direction as well as the right and left (Photo 18-5).

Photo 18-6

Movement 6:

Repeat Movements 3, reversing the facing direction as well as the right and left (Photo 18-6).

Posture 19: Needle at Sea Bottom

Photo 19-1　　　　　　　　　　Photo 19-2

Movement 1:

Draw your right foot beside your left, and at the same time, turn your torso to the right (facing west). Guide the right-hand end of the staff downward in a smooth parrying arc, as if making a kayaking stroke, and push the left-hand end of the staff upward and forward above your head to form a vertical shield. Shift your weight onto your right leg, allowing the left toes to rest lightly on the floor for balance. Hold the staff vertically in front of you with both hands creating a strong, upright guarding structure. Maintain an alert posture, ready to respond (Photo 19-1).

Movement 2:

Without pausing, continue the kayaking motion by guiding the right-hand end of the staff in a smooth circular parry from the outside of your right leg, spiraling it backward and around in a full arc. Allow the right-hand end to swing forward again, pointing west at knee height, while tucking the left-hand portion of the staff firmly under your right armpit, with the tail extending behind your right shoulder for optimal control. At the same time, step your left foot slightly forward, keeping only the ball of the foot on the ground to form a poised and stable left empty stance. As you transition into this position, bend your torso slightly forward and sweep your left palm downward beside your left knee in a low protective parry. This fluid, integrated motion combines spiral energy with structural precision, reinforcing both defensive move and the offensive pecking strike (Photo 19-2).

Posture 20: Fan Through the Back

Photo 20-1   Photo 20-2

Movement 1:

Straighten your torso as you draw your left foot back beside your right, keeping the toes gently touching the floor to maintain balance. Simultaneously, release the staff from under your right armpit and re-grasp it with your left hand around the middle section, bringing it into a vertical position in front of your chest. Your right hand now holds the upper section of the staff in front of your forehead, forming a centered and upright guard posture (Photo 20-1).

Movement 2:

Without pausing, rotate your torso to the right (north) and step your left foot forward toward the west, shifting your weight onto it as you settle into a solid left bow stance. As your body aligns, drive the left-hand end of the staff upward and forward at head height toward the west, while simultaneously drawing the right-hand end backward. The motion finishes with the staff held horizontally at forehead level, extending from east to west across your front, channeling both structure and intent (Photo 20-2).

Posture 21: Turn to Deflect, Parry and Punch

Photo 21-1   Photo 21-2

Movement 1:

Shift your weight briefly onto your right foot as you turn your torso to the right, striking the right-hand end of the staff sharply toward the east. At the same time, turn your right toes outward to point toward the northeast, and twist your left heel slightly backward to support the directional change. This coordinated foot adjustment helps facilitate smooth weight transfer while protecting your knees from undue strain during the strike (Photo 21-1).

Movement 2:

Continue by twisting your left heel further back and shifting your weight onto your left foot as you draw your right foot closer. Without interruption, step your right foot out with the toes pointing toward the southeast to form a compact twisting stance. Simultaneously, guide the right-hand end of the staff in a clockwise arc—sweeping downward and then upward toward your right front (southeast)—as if deflecting an incoming weapon. This motion blends rotation, precision, and redirection, preserving your structure while warding off potential threats (Photo 21-2).

Photo 21-3   Photo 21-4

Movement 3:

Step your left foot forward toward the east, but keeping most of your weight on your right leg. At the same time, pull back the right-hand end of the staff to the front of your right hip, and parry the left-hand end of the staff forward in front of your chest pointing to the east (Photo 21-3).

Movement 4:

Shift your weight firmly onto your left foot and slightly draw your right heel back to establish a solid left bow stance. At the same time, drive the staff forward toward the east at upper chest height, maintaining it parallel to the floor for structural alignment and control. The right-hand end of the staff should be securely tucked under your right armpit and braced against your right rib cage, enhancing stability and power transmission. For added momentum and striking force, you may step your left foot slightly farther forward, allowing your lower body to contribute to the forward energy of the strike. This movement emphasizes whole-body coordination and explosive yet grounded delivery (Photo 21-4).

Note: Movement 2, 3, and 4—Deflect, Parry, and Punch—can be combined into one seamless, flowing sequence. As soon as you step your right foot out and deflect the right-hand end of the staff toward your right front (southeast), let that momentum carry you forward as you spring your left foot toward the east. While doing so, parry the left-hand end of the staff to your center front, aligning it with your chest. Without hesitation, follow through with a powerful eastward strike, driving the staff forward at upper chest height. This continuous motion not only builds your reflexes, but also conditions your body to move with integrated speed, structural clarity, and coordinated precision.

Posture 22: Apparent Closure

Photo 22-1   Photo 22-2

Movement 1:

Parry the outer end of the staff upward in a counterclockwise vertical half-circle in front of your face, raising the left-hand end while keeping the right-hand end low. Simultaneously, draw your left foot back close to your right foot to form a compact, balanced stance. Hold the staff vertically in front of your chest with both hands, creating a strong ward-off posture facing east (Photo 22-1).

Movement 2:

Then, root your weight firmly onto your right leg and lift your left heel slightly off the floor for lightness and readiness. As you do this, twist the staff in front of your face clockwise, transitioning it into a horizontal position just above your chest. Roll it backward slightly in a protective arc above your head, keeping both elbows gently bent to maintain flexibility and responsiveness (Photo 22-2).

Photo 22-3

Movement 3:

Step your left foot forward toward the east and shift your weight onto it, settling into a grounded left bow stance. As you move, press the staff downward in front of your chest in a controlled motion, then push it forward to the east at shoulder height. Maintain relaxed shoulders, slightly sunken elbows, and outward-rounded arms to project stable ward-off energy and structural integrity. This posture channels power through the whole body while ensuring balance and readiness (Photo 22-3).

Posture 23: Cross Hands

Photo 23-1   Photo 23-2

Movement 1:

Sink your hips and bend your right knee, turning your torso to the right as you shift your center of gravity toward your right leg into a right leg-weighted horse stance. As your torso rotates, allow your left hand to release the staff, and use your right hand to whip the staff toward the west, following the momentum generated by your body's rotation. At the same time, turn your left toes slightly inward and angle your right heel inward to enhance root and alignment. Let your left arm continue its flow with the turning torso, settling in front of your chest with the palm facing downward for balance and structure (Photo 23-1).

Movement 2:

Without pausing, allow the momentum to carry the staff in a sweeping arc behind your back (north), and raise your right hand above your head to twirl the staff so the outer end points to the east. Simultaneously, parry your left palm in front of your right armpit toward the west, providing both a defensive cover and counterbalance to the east side extended staff. This coordinated motion expresses spiraling control, spatial awareness, and full-body integration (Photo 23-2).

Photo 23-3

Photo23-4

Movement 3:

Lower your right hand and bring the staff down in front of your chest, then join your left hand to grasp the middle section, forming a steady two-handed grip. Position the staff parallel to the floor at chest height, with the left-hand end pointing directly to the east. Maintain upright posture and focus your gaze toward the east, preparing for the next movement with calm precision and structural clarity (Photo 23-3).

Movement 4:

Shift your weight firmly onto your left leg, transitioning into a strong and rooted left bow stance. Thrust the left-hand end of the staff straight forward toward the east with focused intent. Simultaneously, slide your right hand toward the tail end of the staff to extend your reach, maximizing the thrust's range and power. Ensure that the staff remains level, and your shoulders relaxed to maintain balance and penetrating strength in the motion (Photo 23-4).

Posture 24: Closing Form

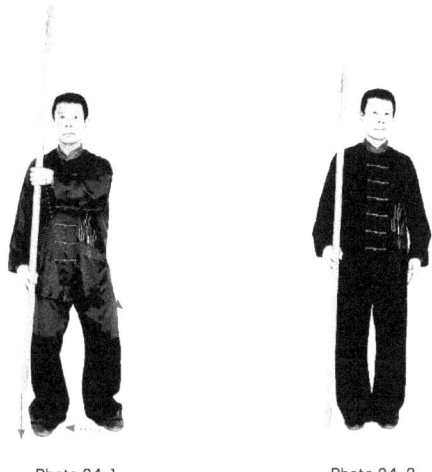

Photo 24-1 Photo 24-2

Movement 1:

Shift your weight onto your right leg and draw your left foot in toward your right, leaving a shoulder-width distance between your feet for stability. As you move, lift the outer (left-hand) end of the staff from its extended position in the east, guiding it upward through a wide arc overhead. Bring the staff into a vertical posture in front of your right shoulder, allowing the right-hand end to drop naturally downward in alignment with your right leg (Photo 24-1).

Movement 2:

Gently lower the right-hand end of the staff to touch the floor just beside your right pinky toe. At the same time, release your left hand from the staff and let it relax down beside your left hip in a composed and grounded posture. The staff should now be held vertically by your right hand, aligned in front of your right shoulder. Finally, bring your left foot next to your right foot, heels together, to return to a neutral standing position and formally complete the routine with poise and presence (Photo 24-2).

―簡化24式太極拳編纂、その前後の歩み― 1

李老師41才（1955年）国家体育運動委員会武術研究室、後に武術処に、ハルビンより転属。これを機会に武術と太極拳の理論と研究、そして組織化のため努力。中でも、今日世界で愛好される簡化二十四式太極拳の編集に取り組み、苦心の結果、教材の掛図（別添参考）とテキストを完成発表（1956年）。その後、日本へ歴史的な経緯を経て、今や、アジア大会エキシビジョン表演など世界に普及される。

24式を編集する時の李老師

1955年，中國北京，傳奇宗師李天驥潛心編創簡化太極二十四式，一筆一劃，凝練千年武道，化繁為簡，傳世留芳。

Legendary Li Tianji working on the design of Simplified Tai Chi Form 24 in 1955, Beijing, China

凝練千年武道, 化繁為簡

Distilling a thousand years of martial wisdom, transforming complexity into simplicity

Supplement

Simplified Tai Chi Form 24 Wall Chart
簡化太極拳掛圖 *1956*

Note: This wall chart was compiled by the General Administration of Sports of China 中國國家體育總局編 and published by People's Sports Publishing House, Beijing, China, 1956 人民體育出版社

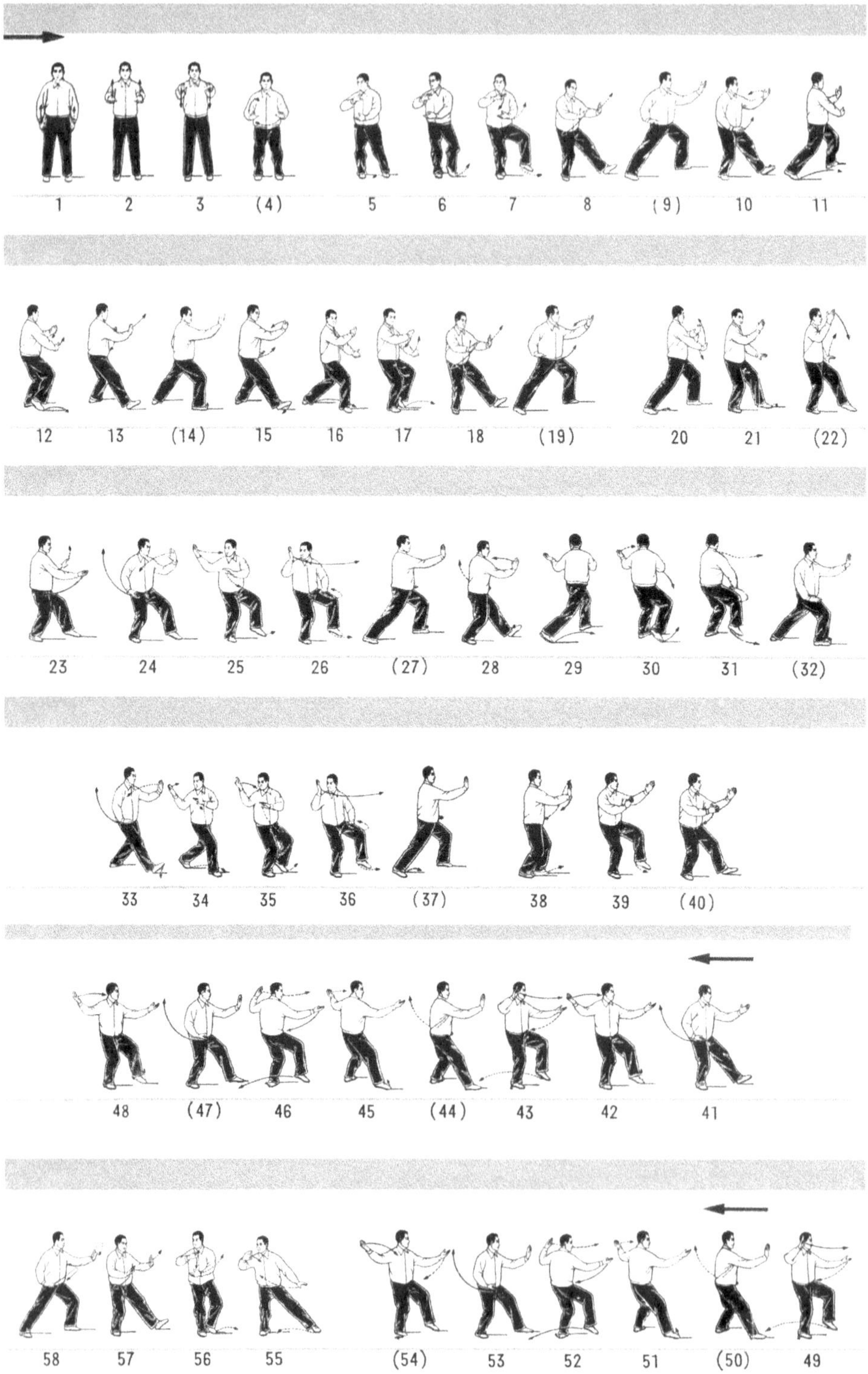
1 2 3 (4) 5 6 7 8 (9) 10 11
12 13 (14) 15 16 17 18 (19) 20 21 (22)
23 24 25 26 (27) 28 29 30 31 (32)
33 34 35 36 (37) 38 39 (40)
48 (47) 46 45 (44) 43 42 41
58 57 56 55 (54) 53 52 51 (50) 49

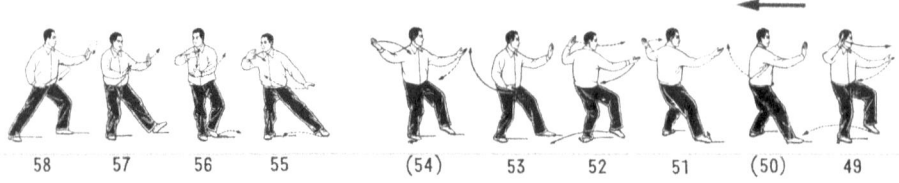

Supplement – Simplified Tai Chi Form 24 Wall Chart

Dr. Jesse Tsao

125　(124)　123　122　121　120　119

134　133　132　(131)　130　129　128　127　126

(144)　143　142　141　140　139　(138)　137　136　135

(154)　153　152　(151)　150　(149)　148　147　146　145

155　156　156反面　157　157反面　158　159　160　(161)　162　163

164　165　166　(167)　168　169　170　(171)　172　173

232

About the Author

Jesse Tsao PhD, born in Penglai, Shandong Province, China (中国蓬莱), is an internationally recognized Tai Chi master, Qigong therapist, alternative medicine expert, and wellness consultant. He is the founder of Tai Chi Healthways, an organization dedicated to promoting health and well-being through Tai Chi and Qigong.

With over fifty years of practice, Dr. Tsao began his Tai Chi journey at the age of seven in his hometown. His lifelong dedication includes ten years of intensive study under Grandmaster Li Deyin 李德印,北京中国人民大学 in Beijing, and he has been a gold medalist in the Beijing Collegiate Wushu Competition in 1980. Dr. Tsao holds the prestigious title of 12th-generation direct- lineage holder of Chen family Tai Chi, solidifying his expertise in one of the most respected traditional Chinese martial arts systems.

Dr. Tsao first brought his Tai Chi expertise to the United States in 1987, when he conducted a Tai Chi workshop in Tucson, Arizona. His passion for the practice eventually led him to leave his initial career as an economist in 1995, focusing fully on

Tai Chi research and teaching. From 1996 to 2015, he served as the chief Tai Chi master for Arizona State employee worksite wellness programs, where he helped countless individuals benefit from his teachings. His unique creation, Tai Chi Bang: Eight Immortal Flute, became so popular that it was offered as an accredited course by the Open College Network in the United Kingdom's Somerset Skill & Learning. His book, Practical Tai Chi Training: A 9-Stage Method for Mastery, was an Amazon Best Seller in 2021.

Specializing in self-healing, preventive therapies, stress management, and mind-body wellness, Dr. Tsao combines traditional Tai Chi wisdom with modern wellness practices. His training is a rare blend of traditional, intense, hands-on martial arts experience and formal academic education. He earned his PhD in Traditional Chinese Martial Arts Education from Shanghai University of Sport in 2013. His knowledge has been further shaped by countless international workshops, seminars, and collaborations with Grandmasters like Chen Xiaowang 陈小旺, Zhu Tiancai 朱天才, and Su Zhifang 蘇自芳. Dr. Tsao's lineage teacher, Grandmaster Chen Zhenglei 陳正雷, is one of the top ten martial artists in China, who passed on to him the traditional Chen family Tai Chi forms.

Beyond his direct training, Dr. Tsao has sought out lessons from many renowned masters in the world of Tai Chi and Wushu, expanding his knowledge and skill set through personal meetings with experts such as Abraham Liu, Dan Lee, and Jet Li's coach Wu Bin. His influence and mastery extend worldwide through his annual international teaching tours since 2005.

Dr. Tsao's contributions to Tai Chi have been acknowledged globally. He was recognized as an Ambassador for Peace and awarded the Hellenic Wushu Federation Honor Award in Greece in 2018. After a twenty-one-year tenure as a health education consultant and Tai Chi master for CIGNA Healthcare in Arizona, Dr. Tsao relocated to San Diego, where he has continued to train Tai Chi instructors through his rigorous certification program. He has produced over 108 instructional DVDs on Tai Chi, Qigong, and health-related practices, and his publications have been translated into Spanish and Hungarian.

Through Tai Chi Healthways, Dr. Tsao continues to inspire students worldwide with his deep knowledge and passion for holistic wellness. His journey symbolizes the perfect fusion of traditional Chinese martial arts and modern health practices.

To learn more, visit taichihealthways.com.

www.ingramcontent.com/pod-product-compliance
Lightning Source LLC
Chambersburg PA
CBHW070642160426
43194CB00009B/1547